BARBADOS T[...] GUIDE BOOK

Barbados Unveiled: Unlocking the Secrets of the Caribbean's Most Captivating Destination - Your Comprehensive Travel Guide for 2023 and Beyond

Kian Wright

DISCLAIMER

This book is a work of fiction. Names, characters, places, and incidents either are the product of the author's imagination or are used fictitiously. Any resemblance to actual persons, living or dead, events, or locales is entirely coincidental.

Copyright © 2023 by Kian Wright

All rights reserved. No part of this book may be reproduced, scanned, or distributed in any printed or electronic form without permission. Please do not participate in or encourage piracy of copyrighted materials in violation of the author's rights. Purchase only authorized editions.

This book is licensed for your enjoyment only. It may not be re-sold or given away to other people. If you would like to share this book with another person, please purchase an additional copy for each recipient. If you're reading this book and did not purchase it, or it was not purchased for your use only, then please return it to your favourite bookseller and purchase your copy. Thank you for respecting the hard work of this author.

This book is published by Kian Wright, and all rights are reserved by the publisher.

Disclaimer

The information contained in this book is for general information purposes only.

The information is provided by the author and while we endeavour to keep the information up to date and correct, we make no representations or warranties of any kind, express or implied, about the completeness, accuracy, reliability, suitability, or availability concerning the book or the information, products, services, or related graphics contained in the book for any purpose. Any reliance you place on such information is therefore strictly at your own risk. In no event will the author or publisher be liable for any loss or damage including without limitation, indirect or consequential loss or damage, or any loss or damage whatsoever arising from loss of data or profits arising out of, or in connection with, the use of this Book.

Please note that this disclaimer is subject to change without notice.

TABLE OF CONTENT

Maps and directions to explore anywhere in Barbados with accommodation options available and the best place to stay 3
Itinerary options to explore Barbados based on your desired length of stay 3
A day trip in Barbados 3
Museums and galleries to visit in Barbados 3
Festivals and Events 3
Outdoor Adventures in Barbados 3
Shopping and Souvenirs in Barbados 3
Barbados Nightlife and Entertainment 3
Best place to eat, drink and chop in Barbados 3
Water sports and Activities in Barbados 3
How to live on a budget in Barbados 3
Safety and health information 3
Introduction 1

Introduction

Barbados, located in the eastern Caribbean, is a vibrant island country known for its stunning beaches, rich history, friendly locals, and diverse culture.
Here's a detailed introduction to help you explore everything about Barbados:
Geography and Climate:
Barbados is situated in the Lesser Antilles, bordered by the Atlantic Ocean to the east and the Caribbean Sea to the west. The island is relatively flat with gently rolling hills, and its coastline is dotted with beautiful beaches, rocky cliffs, and picturesque bays. The climate in Barbados is tropical, with warm temperatures year-round. The dry season typically runs from December to May, while the wet season occurs from June to November, with a higher chance of rainfall and occasional tropical storms.
Culture and People:

Barbados boasts a rich cultural heritage influenced by African, British, and West Indian traditions. Bajans, as the locals are known, are warm, friendly, and proud of their island's history. The island's official language is English, and the Bajan dialect, a unique blend of English and African languages, is commonly spoken. The vibrant culture is reflected in the island's music, dance, festivals, and culinary traditions, including the famous flying fish and cou-cou dish.

History and Landmarks:

Barbados has a fascinating history shaped by colonization and the sugar industry. The island was first settled by the indigenous Arawak and Carib peoples, later colonized by the British, and gained independence in 1966.

Historic landmarks and sites worth visiting include:

Bridgetown and its Garrison: A UNESCO World Heritage Site, featuring colonial architecture, historical buildings like the Parliament Buildings, and the impressive Garrison area, which was once a British military base.

St. Nicholas Abbey: A beautifully restored plantation house dating back to the 17th century, offering a glimpse into Barbados' sugar plantation era.

George Washington House: The only house outside the United States where the first U.S. President, George Washington, stayed.

Morgan Lewis Windmill: One of the only two intact sugar windmills in the Caribbean, offering panoramic views of the countryside.

Barbados Museum & Historical Society: Housed in the former British Military Prison, the museum exhibits artefacts and exhibits showcasing the island's history and culture.

Beaches and Water Activities:

Barbados is renowned for its stunning beaches with crystal-clear turquoise waters and powdery white sand.

Some of the most popular beaches include:

Crane Beach: Located on the southeast coast, known for its picturesque setting and dramatic cliffs.

Accra Beach: Situated on the south coast, offering calm waters and a vibrant atmosphere with beachfront restaurants and bars.

Carlisle Bay : A picturesque bay with calm waters, perfect for snorkelling and diving, and home to several shipwrecks and vibrant marine life.

Bottom Bay: A secluded and picturesque beach on the southeast coast, surrounded by towering cliffs.

Water activities in Barbados include snorkelling, scuba diving, sailing, jet skiing, paddle boarding, and catamaran cruises. The island's warm waters and diverse marine life provide ample opportunities for exploration and adventure.

Cuisine:

Barbadian cuisine, often referred to as Bajan cuisine, is a fusion of African, British, and West Indian flavours. Some must-try dishes include flying fish and cou-cou (a national dish), macaroni pie, pepperpot stew, and fish cakes. Bajan cuisine is known for its bold flavours and the use of local ingredients such as fresh seafood, tropical fruits, and spices like nutmeg and allspice.

Festivals and Events:

Barbados is famous for its colourful festivals and vibrant celebrations. The Crop Over Festival, held The Crop Over Festival, held annually from June to August, is Barbados' biggest and most popular festival. It originated from the time when sugar cane was the island's main crop, and it celebrates the end of the sugar cane harvest season. The festival features a variety of events, including calypso music competitions, colourful parades, traditional dancing, art exhibitions, craft markets, and the crowning of the King and Queen of the Crop. The grand finale, called Grand Kadooment, is a massive street parade where revellers dressed in elaborate costumes dance through the streets of Bridgetown.

Another significant event in Barbados is the Oistins Fish Festival, held over the Easter weekend. It takes place in the lively fishing village of Oistins and showcases the island's fishing heritage. Visitors can sample an array of delicious seafood dishes, enjoy live music performances, watch fishing boat races, and experience the lively and festive atmosphere.

Barbados also hosts various sporting events that attract participants and spectators from around the world. The Barbados Golf Open, Barbados Reggae Festival, Mount Gay Rum Round Barbados Race, and the Barbados International Surfing Festival are just a few examples of sporting and cultural events that take place throughout the year.

Nature and Outdoor Activities:

Barbados offers a range of natural attractions and outdoor activities to explore its scenic beauty.

Some notable places and activities include:

Harrison's Cave: A magnificent underground cave system with stalactites, stalagmites, and crystallized formations. Visitors can take tram tours through the cave to admire its natural wonders.

Animal Flower Cave: Located on the northern tip of the island, this sea cave offers breathtaking views of the Atlantic Ocean and houses pools filled with colourful sea anemones, hence its name.

Barbados Wildlife Reserve: A sanctuary for local wildlife, including green monkeys, tortoises, and a variety of bird species. Visitors can stroll through the reserve and observe the animals in their natural habitat.

Andromeda Botanic Gardens: Situated on the east coast, these gardens showcase a diverse collection of tropical plants, flowers, and trees. It is a tranquil spot for nature lovers and offers stunning views of the coastline.

Hiking and Nature Trails: Barbados has a network of scenic hiking trails that traverse lush forests, coastal cliffs, and picturesque landscapes. Some popular trails include Welchman Hall Gully, Farley Hill National Park, and the Scotland District Hiking Trail.

These are just a few highlights of what Barbados has to offer. The island's warm hospitality, stunning natural beauty, vibrant culture, and range of activities make it an ideal destination for travellers seeking a mix of relaxation, adventure, and cultural exploration. Whether it's lounging on the beautiful beaches, immersing in the island's rich history, enjoying water sports, or indulging in delicious cuisine, Barbados has something for everyone to enjoy and create lasting memories.

Maps and directions to explore anywhere in Barbados with accommodation options available and the best place to stay

Popular Discounts
Kendal Hill
Grantley Adams International Airport
Recently viewed
Oistins
Silver Sands Beach
Cane Vale

Flatfield
Speightstown
SAINT PETER
Mount Standfast
Holetown
H1
Fitts Village
Belleplaine
H2
Bridgetown
Bathsheba
H3
Barbados
H4
SAINT JOHN
H6
Oistins
Six Cross Roads
Marley Vale
H5

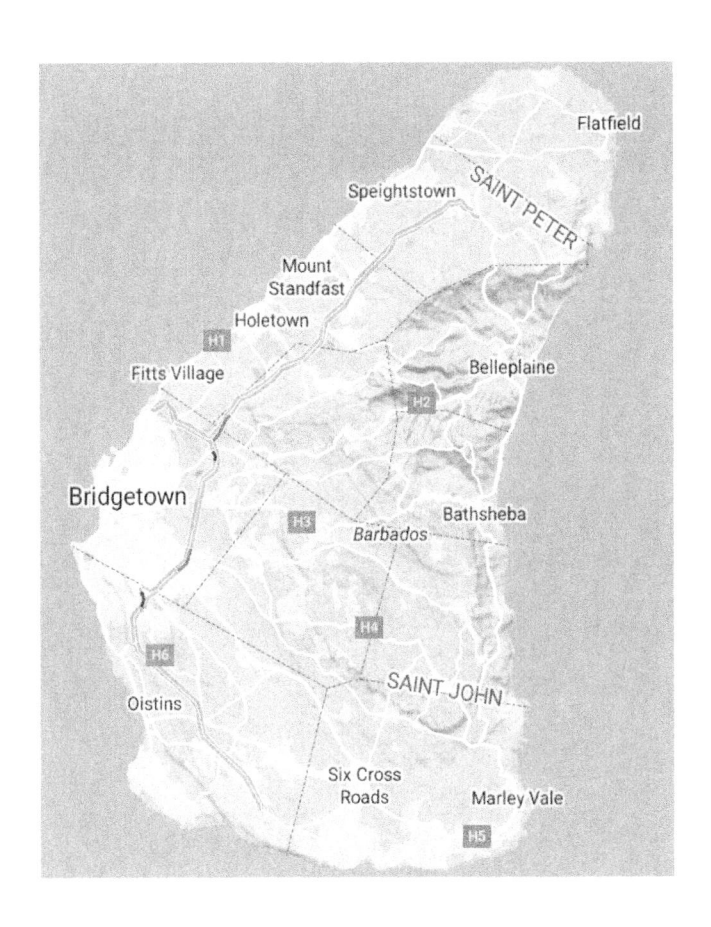

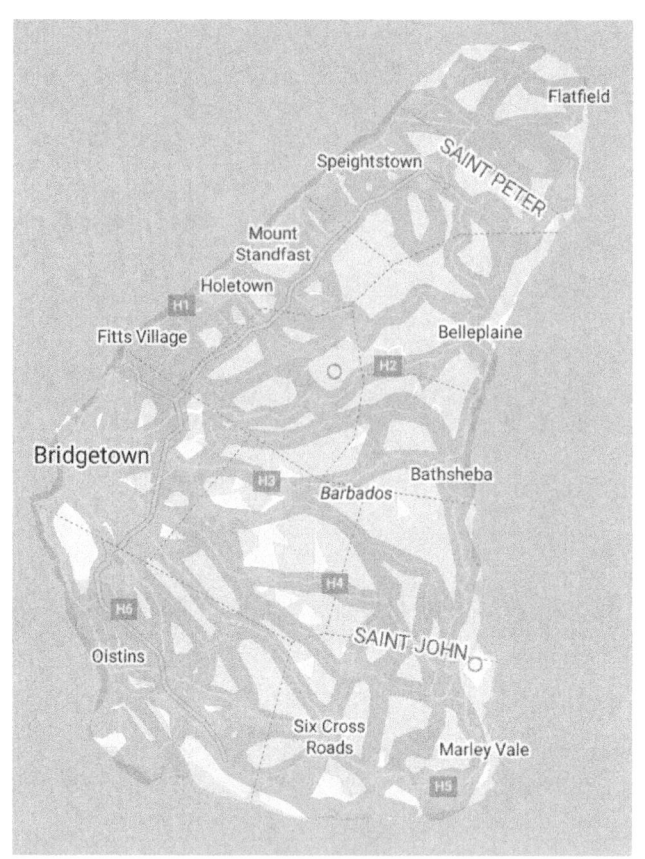

How to get to Barbados:
Most people go to Barbados via plane or water. Grantley Adams International Airport (BGI), which is situated near Seawell, Christ Church, is the primary international entry point. Many airlines fly directly to it from different places across the world.

Major carriers like American Airlines, British Airways, Air Canada, JetBlue Airways, and Virgin Atlantic offer flights to Barbados. For the most recent information on flight availability and timetables, it is advised to check with the airlines or travel agencies.

Barbados is a preferred cruise location for tourists who love to travel by sea. The main cruise port is the Bridgetown Port, which is situated in Bridgetown's capital.

Numerous cruise lines provide itineraries including Barbados as a port of call.

Grantley Adams International Airport (BGI) is the primary airport in Barbados where most passengers will arrive. It is the main international entry point into the nation and is situated in Seawell, Christ Church. The Grantley Adams International Airport has all the amenities and services necessary to meet the requirements of visitors.

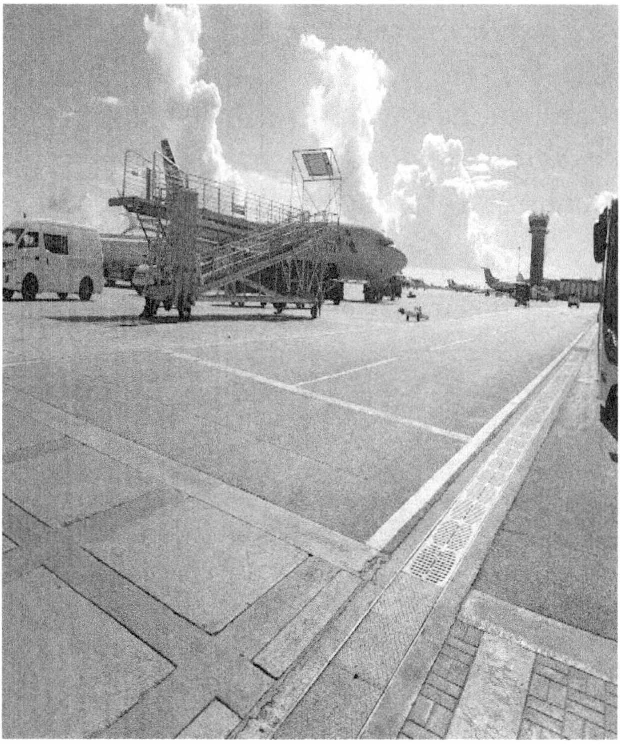

Visitors can choose from a variety of alternatives for exploring various locations in Barbados after arriving at Grantley Adams International Airport:

Taxis:

Taxis are a convenient way to get where you're going and are widely accessible at the airport. You may find authorised taxis at a designated taxi stop outside the arrivals area. Before setting off on your excursion, it is recommended to confirm the fare with the driver.

Car Rental:

Rent a car from one of the car rental companies at the airport if you'd like greater freedom and independence while touring Barbados. You can use your automobile to travel to other locations in your own time thanks to this. Before you get behind the wheel, don't forget to verify the local traffic laws and bring your driver's licence.

Using Public Transit:
Buses and minibuses, or "ZR vans," are the primary modes of transportation in Barbados. You can ride buses or ZR vans to get to various parts of the island; the bus terminal is close to the airport. Most areas are serviced by bus routes, which are also an inexpensive choice for transportation.

Following arrival and selection of your mode of transportation, check out some of Barbados' most well-known destinations:

Bridgetown:

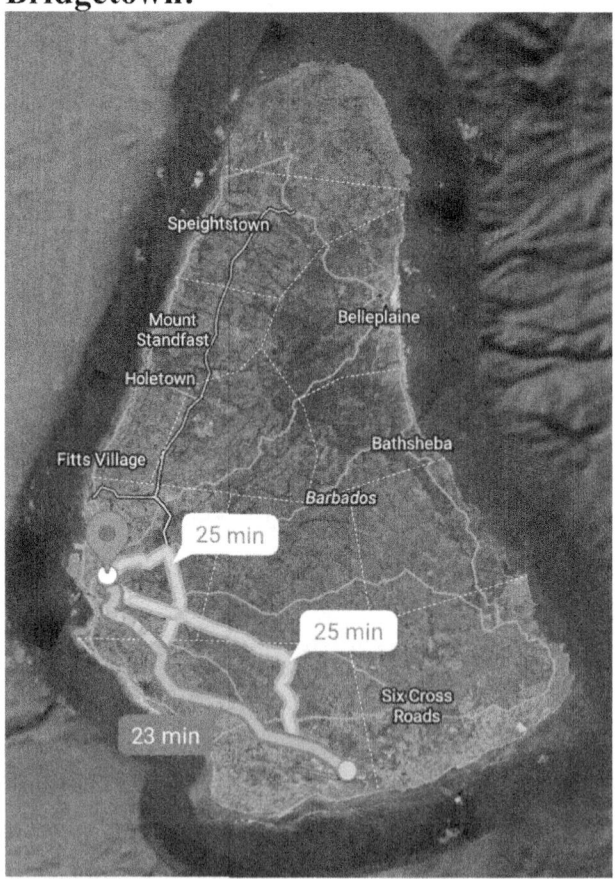

Grantley Adams International Airport (BGI) to Bridgetown

23 min (16 km)
Fastest route now due to traffic conditions

Steps

◉ Grantley Adams International Airport, Adams-Barrow, Gordon Cummins Hwy, Barbados

↑ Head west on Airport Access Rd toward S Ramp
400 m

↱ Turn right toward Tom Adams Hwy
50 m

↰ Turn left onto Tom Adams Hwy
1.8 km

⥁ At the roundabout, take the 1st exit and stay on Tom Adams Hwy
30 m

⤓ Exit the roundabout onto Tom Adams Hwy
2.6 km

⥁ At the roundabout, take the 1st exit and stay on Tom Adams Hwy

Step 1

↑ Exit the roundabout onto Tom Adams Hwy

3.1 km

↻ At the roundabout, take the 2nd exit and stay on Tom Adams Hwy

60 m

↑ Exit the roundabout onto Tom Adams Hwy

1.2 km

↻ At the roundabout, take the 2nd exit onto Errol Barrow Hwy

90 m

↑ Exit the roundabout onto Errol Barrow Hwy

1.6 km

↻ At the roundabout, take the 2nd exit and stay on Errol Barrow Hwy

30 m

↑ Exit the roundabout onto Errol Barrow Hwy

800 m

Step 2

↱ Keep left to continue on Wildey Main Rd/ Hwy 6
   ⓘ Continue to follow Hwy 6
   2.7 km

↻ At the roundabout, take the 3rd exit onto Martindales Rd
   700 m

↻ At the roundabout, continue straight onto Halls Rd
   450 m

↺ At the roundabout, take the 1st exit onto Roebuck St
   50 m

⚐ Exit the roundabout onto Roebuck St
   350 m

↱ Turn right onto Country Rd
   550 m

◉ Bridgetown
   Barbados

Final step
Visit Barbados' capital city, which is renowned for its historical buildings, popular shopping district, and landmarks including the Parliament Buildings and Barbados Museum & Historical Society.
West Coast:

Grantley Adams International Airport (BGI) to West Coast

33 min ↑ (27 km)

Fastest route now due to traffic conditions, but it's getting worse

9:00 AM   10:00 AM   11:00 AM

Steps

⊙ Grantley Adams International Airport, Adams-Barrow, Gordon Cummins Hwy, Barbados

↑ Head west on Airport Access Rd toward S Ramp

400 m

↱ Turn right toward Tom Adams Hwy

50 m

↰ Turn left onto Tom Adams Hwy

1.8 km

↻ At the roundabout, take the 1st exit and stay on Tom Adams Hwy

30 m

↗ Exit the roundabout onto Tom Adams Hwy

2.6 km

Step 1

17

At the roundabout, take the 1st exit and stay on Tom Adams Hwy

20 m

Exit the roundabout onto Tom Adams Hwy

3.1 km

At the roundabout, take the 2nd exit and stay on Tom Adams Hwy

60 m

Exit the roundabout onto Tom Adams Hwy

1.2 km

At the roundabout, take the 2nd exit onto Errol Barrow Hwy

90 m

Exit the roundabout onto Errol Barrow Hwy

1.6 km

At the roundabout, take the 2nd exit and stay on Errol Barrow Hwy

30 m

Step 2

↱　Exit the roundabout onto Errol Barrow Hwy

　　800 m

↱　Sharp right to stay on Errol Barrow Hwy

　　700 m

↗　Keep right to stay on Errol Barrow Hwy

　　80 m

↺　At the roundabout, take the 1st exit and stay on Errol Barrow Hwy

　　30 m

↱　Exit the roundabout onto Errol Barrow Hwy

　　1.1 km

↺　At the roundabout, take the 2nd exit and stay on Errol Barrow Hwy

　　60 m

↱　Exit the roundabout onto Errol Barrow Hwy

　　1.0 km

↺　At the roundabout, take the 2nd exit and stay on Errol Barrow Hwy

Step 3

Exit the roundabout onto Errol Barrow Hwy

1.9 km

At the roundabout, take the 1st exit and stay on Errol Barrow Hwy

50 m

Exit the roundabout onto Errol Barrow Hwy

2.2 km

At the roundabout, take the 2nd exit and stay on Errol Barrow Hwy

60 m

Exit the roundabout onto Errol Barrow Hwy

350 m

At the roundabout, take the 3rd exit onto Hwy 2A/Ronald Mapp Hwy

90 m

Exit the roundabout onto Hwy 2A/Ronald Mapp Hwy

1.3 km

Step 4

	At the roundabout, take the 2nd exit and stay on Hwy 2A/Ronald Mapp Hwy
	50 m
	Exit the roundabout onto Hwy 2A/Ronald Mapp Hwy
	800 m
	At the roundabout, take the 1st exit and stay on Hwy 2A/Ronald Mapp Hwy
	3.0 km
	At the roundabout, take the 1st exit onto Hwy 1A/Sea View
	30 m
	Exit the roundabout onto Hwy 1A/Sea View
	2.8 km
	West Coast Taxi Service Barbados 2nd Street
	Destination will be on the left

Final step

Discover the legendary Platinum Coast on Barbados' west coast, which offers opulent cuisine, dazzling beaches, and opulent resorts. Places like Holetown, Speightstown, and the quaint town of St. James are worth visiting.

East Coast:

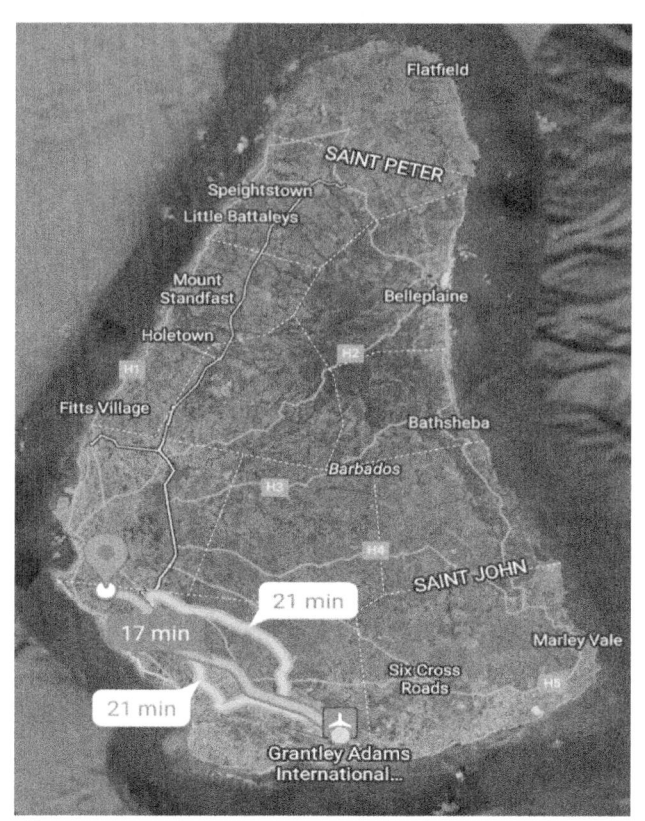

Grantley Adams International Airport (BGI) to East Coast

17 min (13 km)

Fastest route now due to traffic conditions

Steps

⊙ Grantley Adams International Airport, Adams-Barrow, Gordon Cummins Hwy, Barbados

↑ Head west on Airport Access Rd toward S Ramp
400 m

↱ Turn right toward Tom Adams Hwy
50 m

↰ Turn left onto Tom Adams Hwy
1.8 km

⤺ At the roundabout, take the 1st exit and stay on Tom Adams Hwy
30 m

↗ Exit the roundabout onto Tom Adams Hwy
2.6 km

↗ At the roundabout, take the 1st exit and stay on Tom Adams Hwy

Step 1

- Exit the roundabout onto Tom Adams Hwy

    3.1 km

- At the roundabout, take the 2nd exit and stay on Tom Adams Hwy

    60 m

- Exit the roundabout onto Tom Adams Hwy

    1.2 km

- At the roundabout, take the 2nd exit onto Errol Barrow Hwy

    90 m

- Exit the roundabout onto Errol Barrow Hwy

    1.6 km

- At the roundabout, take the 1st exit onto Rendezvous Hill

    20 m

- Exit the roundabout onto Rendezvous Hill

    160 m

- Turn right onto Forde's Rd

Step 2

↰ At the roundabout, take the 1st exit onto Rendezvous Hill

20 m

↗ Exit the roundabout onto Rendezvous Hill

160 m

↱ Turn right onto Forde's Rd

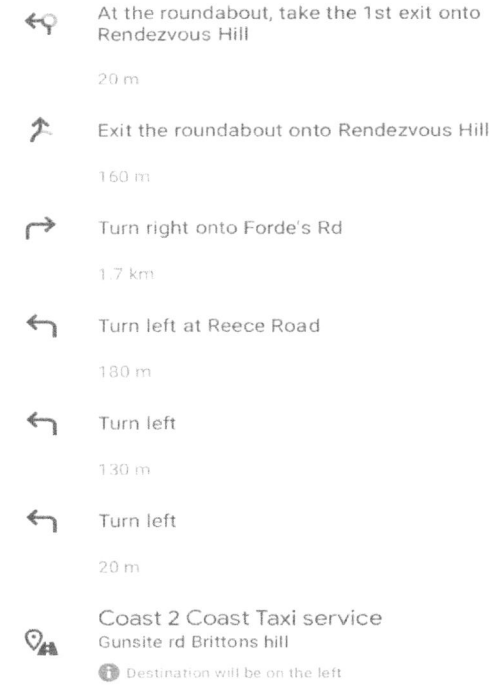

1.7 km

↰ Turn left at Reece Road

180 m

↰ Turn left

130 m

↰ Turn left

20 m

📍 Coast 2 Coast Taxi service
Gunsite rd Brittons hill
ⓘ Destination will be on the left

Final step

Discover the untamed beauty of the east coast, which is renowned for its towering cliffs, raging Atlantic seas, and picture-perfect communities like Bathsheba. It's a fantastic location for hiking, surfing, and picturesque drives.

The South Coast:

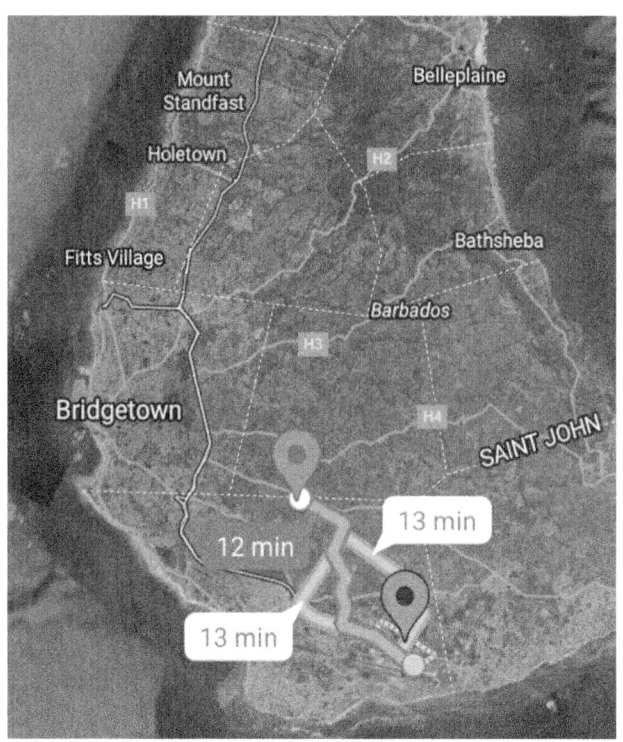

Grantley Adams International Airport (BGI) to the South Coast

12 min (9.1 km)

Fastest route now due to traffic conditions

Steps

- ◉ Grantley Adams International Airport, Adams-Barrow, Gordon Cummins Hwy, Barbados

- ↑ Head west on Airport Access Rd toward S Ramp

  400 m

- ↱ Turn right toward Tom Adams Hwy

  50 m

- ↰ Turn left onto Tom Adams Hwy

  1.8 km

- ⟳ At the roundabout, take the 1st exit and stay on Tom Adams Hwy

  30 m

- ✈ Exit the roundabout onto Tom Adams Hwy

  800 m

Step 1

12 min (9.1 km)
Fastest route now due to traffic conditions

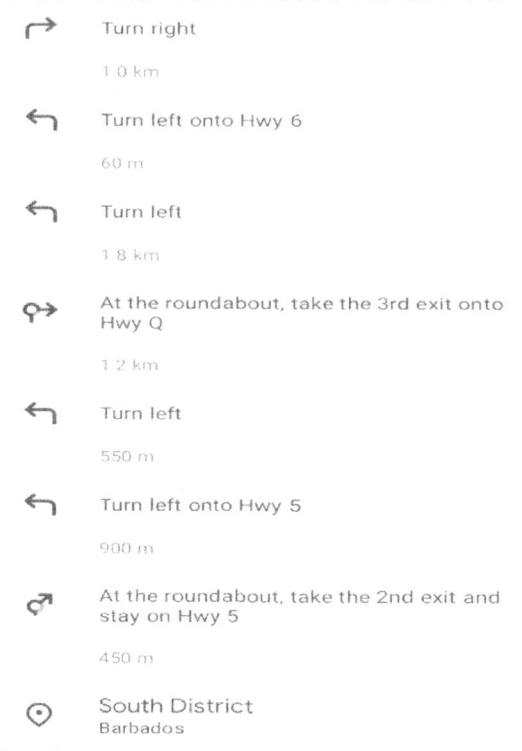

↱ Turn right
1.0 km

↰ Turn left onto Hwy 6
60 m

↰ Turn left
1.8 km

⊙→ At the roundabout, take the 3rd exit onto Hwy Q
1.2 km

↰ Turn left
550 m

↰ Turn left onto Hwy 5
900 m

⊙↗ At the roundabout, take the 2nd exit and stay on Hwy 5
450 m

⊙ South District
Barbados

Final step
Discover the exciting south coast, which offers a variety of stunning beaches, a thriving nightlife, water sports, and a selection of lodging and dining options.
The North Coast:

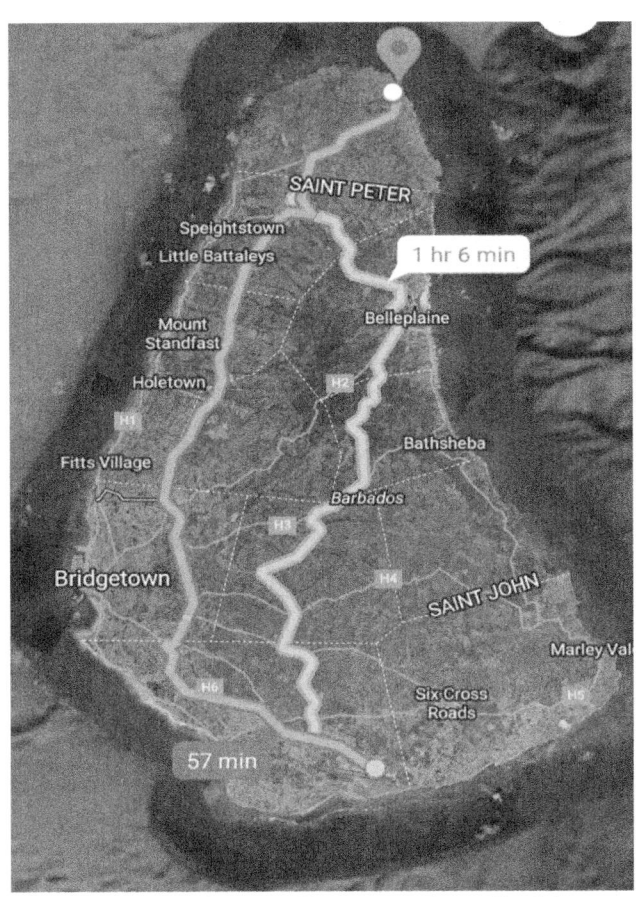

Grantley Adams International Airport (BGI) to the North Coast

57 min (43 km)

Fastest route now due to traffic conditions

Steps

⊙ Grantley Adams International Airport, Adams-Barrow, Gordon Cummins Hwy, Barbados

↑ Head west on Airport Access Rd toward S Ramp

400 m

↱ Turn right toward Tom Adams Hwy

50 m

↰ Turn left onto Tom Adams Hwy

1.8 km

At the roundabout, take the 1st exit and stay on Tom Adams Hwy

30 m

Exit the roundabout onto Tom Adams Hwy

2.6 km

At the roundabout, take the 1st exit and stay on Tom Adams Hwy

Step 1

- Exit the roundabout onto Tom Adams Hwy

  3.1 km

- At the roundabout, take the 2nd exit and stay on Tom Adams Hwy

  60 m

- Exit the roundabout onto Tom Adams Hwy

  1.2 km

- At the roundabout, take the 2nd exit onto Errol Barrow Hwy

  90 m

- Exit the roundabout onto Errol Barrow Hwy

  1.6 km

- At the roundabout, take the 2nd exit and stay on Errol Barrow Hwy

  30 m

- Exit the roundabout onto Errol Barrow Hwy

  800 m

- Sharp right to stay on Errol Barrow Hwy

Step 2

Keep left to continue toward Errol Barrow Hwy

160 m

Merge onto Errol Barrow Hwy

1.0 km

At the roundabout, take the 2nd exit and stay on Errol Barrow Hwy

60 m

Exit the roundabout onto Errol Barrow Hwy

1.0 km

At the roundabout, take the 2nd exit and stay on Errol Barrow Hwy

30 m

Exit the roundabout onto Errol Barrow Hwy

1.9 km

At the roundabout, take the 1st exit and stay on Errol Barrow Hwy

50 m

Exit the roundabout onto Errol Barrow Hwy

Step 3

↻ At the roundabout, take the 1st exit and stay on Errol Barrow Hwy

50 m

↗ Exit the roundabout onto Errol Barrow Hwy

2.2 km

↻ At the roundabout, take the 2nd exit and stay on Errol Barrow Hwy

60 m

↗ Exit the roundabout onto Errol Barrow Hwy

350 m

↻→ At the roundabout, take the 3rd exit onto Hwy 2A/Ronald Mapp Hwy

90 m

↗ Exit the roundabout onto Hwy 2A/Ronald Mapp Hwy

1.3 km

↻ At the roundabout, take the 2nd exit and stay on Hwy 2A/Ronald Mapp Hwy

50 m

Step 4

↗ Exit the roundabout onto Hwy 2A/Ronald Mapp Hwy

800 m

↱ At the roundabout, take the 1st exit and stay on Hwy 2A/Ronald Mapp Hwy

3.0 km

↗ At the roundabout, take the 2nd exit and stay on Hwy 2A/Ronald Mapp Hwy

130 m

↗ Exit the roundabout onto Hwy 2A/Ronald Mapp Hwy

1.7 km

↑ At the roundabout, take the 2nd exit and stay on Hwy 2A/Ronald Mapp Hwy

60 m

↗ Exit the roundabout onto Hwy 2A/Ronald Mapp Hwy

8.9 km

↰ Turn left onto Charles Duncan Oneal Hwy

2.9 km

Step 5

← Turn left onto Charles Duncan Oneal Hwy

2.9 km

↱ At the roundabout, take the 3rd exit

100 m

↥ Exit the roundabout

270 m

↱ Turn right onto Hwy 1C

4.9 km

↱ Turn right

150 m

⊙ North Coast
89JV+M49

Final step
Visit Barbados' north shore to take advantage of the opportunity for beautiful treks, cave exploration, and breathtaking coastal vistas.

A place to stay in Barbados:
Barbados provides a wide variety of lodging choices to suit all tastes and price ranges.

Following are some well-liked lodging types and where they can be found:

Hotels and Resorts:
Sandy Lane Hotel: Situated on the west coast of Barbados in the parish of St. James, the address is Sandy Lane Hotel Sandy Lane St. James, BB24024, Barbados.

Sandy Lane Hotel is a renowned luxury resort located in St. James Parish on the West Coast of Barbados. It offers a range of services and amenities to provide guests with a memorable and indulgent experience. Here are some of the services typically offered by Sandy Lane Hotel:

Accommodations: Sandy Lane Hotel features elegantly appointed rooms, suites, and villas, each offering luxurious amenities and beautiful views. The accommodations are designed to provide comfort and privacy, with features like private balconies or patios, marble bathrooms, and plush furnishings.

Dining: The resort boasts several exceptional dining options, including fine-dining restaurants and casual eateries. Guests can enjoy a variety of culinary experiences, from gourmet international cuisine to local Barbadian specialities. The restaurants at Sandy Lane Hotel are known for their impeccable service and high-quality cuisine.

Spa and Wellness: The resort is home to an award-winning spa that offers a range of treatments and therapies for relaxation and rejuvenation. Guests can indulge in massages, facials, body scrubs, and other wellness services. The spa facilities often include saunas, steam rooms, plunge pools, and relaxation areas.

Golf: Sandy Lane Hotel is renowned for its world-class golf courses. The resort features three golf courses: The Old Nine, The Country Club, and The Green Monkey. Golf enthusiasts can enjoy challenging fairways, breathtaking views, and professional instruction.

Water Sports and Activities: The resort provides various water sports and recreational activities. Guests can partake in snorkelling, paddleboarding, kayaking, and catamaran cruises. The resort also offers tennis courts, fitness facilities, and access to nearby attractions and excursions.

To get to Sandy Lane Hotel, you can fly into Grantley Adams International Airport (BGI) in Barbados. From the airport, you have several transportation options:

Private Transfer: Sandy Lane Hotel can arrange for a private transfer service to pick you up from the airport and take you directly to the resort. This option offers convenience and comfort.

Taxi: Taxis are readily available at the airport, and you can take one to Sandy Lane Hotel. It's advisable to confirm the fare with the driver before getting into the taxi.

Rental Car: If you prefer more flexibility and independence, you can rent a car at the airport and drive to the resort. Barbados has well-maintained roads, and driving is on the left side.

The Spa and pool at sandy lane

The tennis

Map and direction from Grantley Adams International Airport (BGI) to Sandy Lane hotel

Grantley Adams International Airport (BGI) to Sandy Lane Hotel

32 min (26 km)
Fastest route now due to traffic conditions

Steps

⊙ Grantley Adams International Airport

↑ Head west on Airport Access Rd toward S Ramp
400 m

↑ Continue straight
2.6 km

↱ Turn right
300 m

↰ Turn left onto Tom Adams Hwy
1.8 km

⤴ At the roundabout, take the 1st exit and stay on Tom Adams Hwy
20 m

⤴ Exit the roundabout onto Tom Adams Hwy
600 m

Step 1

→ Turn right at Newton Industrial Park

3.3 km

↖ Slight left onto Hwy R

2.0 km

↖ Slight left toward Errol Barrow Hwy

140 m

↑ Continue straight onto Errol Barrow Hwy

160 m

→ Turn right onto Errol Barrow Hwy/Wildey Main Rd

450 m

↱ Sharp right onto Errol Barrow Hwy

700 m

↗ Keep right to stay on Errol Barrow Hwy

80 m

⟳ At the roundabout, take the 1st exit and stay on Errol Barrow Hwy

30 m

Step 2

🏃 Exit the roundabout onto Errol Barrow Hwy

1.1 km

🔄 At the roundabout, take the 2nd exit and stay on Errol Barrow Hwy

60 m

🏃 Exit the roundabout onto Errol Barrow Hwy

1.0 km

🔄 At the roundabout, take the 2nd exit and stay on Errol Barrow Hwy

30 m

🏃 Exit the roundabout onto Errol Barrow Hwy

1.9 km

🔄 At the roundabout, take the 1st exit and stay on Errol Barrow Hwy

50 m

🏃 Exit the roundabout onto Errol Barrow Hwy

2.2 km

🔄 At the roundabout, take the 2nd exit and stay on Errol Barrow Hwy

Step 3

32 min (26 km)

Fastest route now due to traffic conditions

↗ Exit the roundabout onto Errol Barrow Hwy

350 m

↱ At the roundabout, take the 3rd exit onto Hwy 2A/Ronald Mapp Hwy

90 m

↗ Exit the roundabout onto Hwy 2A/Ronald Mapp Hwy

1.3 km

↻ At the roundabout, take the 2nd exit and stay on Hwy 2A/Ronald Mapp Hwy

50 m

↗ Exit the roundabout onto Hwy 2A/Ronald Mapp Hwy

800 m

↱ At the roundabout, take the 1st exit and stay on Hwy 2A/Ronald Mapp Hwy

1.5 km

↰ Turn left onto Molyneux Rd

2.7 km

Step 4

↰ Turn left onto Hwy 1

400 m

◉ Sandy Lane Hotel

Sandy Lane Hotel Sandy Lane St. James

Final step

The Crane Resort: Located on the southeast coast in the parish of St. Philip, the address is The Crane, St. Philip.

The Crane Resort is a luxurious property situated on the East Coast of Barbados. It is known for its stunning beachfront location and upscale amenities. Here are some of the services typically offered by The Crane Resort:

Accommodations: The resort features a variety of accommodations, including suites, penthouses, and private residences. These accommodations are elegantly designed and equipped with modern amenities. Many of them offer breathtaking ocean views and private plunge pools.

Dining: The Crane Resort offers a selection of dining options, including several restaurants and bars. Guests can indulge in a range of cuisines, from Caribbean-inspired dishes to international favourites. The resort's restaurants often provide scenic views and a refined dining experience.

Beach and Pools: The resort boasts a beautiful beach with soft sand and turquoise waters. Guests can relax on lounge chairs, soak up the sun, and take refreshing dips in the ocean. Additionally, The Crane Resort has multiple pools, including cascading pools overlooking the cliffs and a stunning infinity pool.

Spa and Wellness: The resort features a spa that offers a variety of treatments, massages, and therapies. Guests can enjoy pampering experiences, rejuvenating massages, and beauty services. The spa facilities often include relaxation areas, steam rooms, and plunge pools.

Fitness and Activities: The Crane Resort provides fitness facilities, including a well-equipped gym. Additionally, the resort offers various activities such as yoga classes, tennis courts, and water sports like snorkelling and kayaking.

To get to The Crane Resort, you can fly into Grantley Adams International Airport (BGI) in Barbados. From the airport, you have several transportation options:

Private Transfer: The Crane Resort can arrange for a private transfer service to pick you up from the airport and take you directly to the resort. This option offers convenience and comfort.

Taxi: Taxis are readily available at the airport, and you can take one to The Crane Resort. It's advisable to confirm the fare with the driver before getting into the taxi.

Rental Car: If you prefer more flexibility and independence, you can rent a car at the airport and drive to the resort. Barbados has well-maintained roads, and driving is on the left side.

Map and direction from Grantley Adams International Airport (BGI) to The Crane Resort

Grantley Adams International Airport (BGI) to the Crane Resort

13 min (7.1 km)

Fastest route now due to traffic conditions

Steps

- ⊙ Grantley Adams International Airport

- ↑ Head west on Airport Access Rd toward S Ramp

  400 m

- ↱ Turn right

  50 m

- ↗ Slight right at Tom Adams Hwy

  40 m

- ↰ Turn left

  350 m

- ↫ At the roundabout, take the 1st exit

  1.3 km

- ↱ Turn right

  2.2 km

Step 1

↱ Turn right onto Headings New Rd/Heddings Main Rd

    🛈 Continue to follow Heddings Main Rd

    1.1 km

↗ Slight right at Heddings New Rd #1

    450 m

↰ Turn left onto Gully Rd

    300 m

↱ Turn right

    750 m

↱ Turn right at Crane Lodge

    50 m

↰ Turn left onto The Crane

    200 m

⊙ The Crane Resort, Barbados
   The Crane Resort

Last step

Fairmont Royal Pavilion: Situated on the west coast in the parish of St. James, the address is Porters, St. James.

Fairmont Royal Pavilion is a luxurious beachfront resort located in St. James Parish on the West Coast of Barbados. Known for its elegant ambience and impeccable service, the resort offers a range of services and amenities to enhance guests' stay. Here are some of the services typically offered by Fairmont Royal Pavilion:

Accommodations: The resort provides spacious and well-appointed rooms and suites, many of which offer breathtaking ocean views. The accommodations are designed to provide comfort and luxury, featuring amenities such as private balconies or terraces, luxurious bathrooms, and high-quality furnishings.

Dining: Fairmont Royal Pavilion offers a variety of dining options, including a beachfront restaurant and a poolside bar. Guests can savour delicious cuisine and enjoy the picturesque views while dining. The resort's restaurants often feature a combination of international flavours and local Barbadian specialities.

Beach and Pools: The resort boasts direct access to a pristine beach, where guests can relax on lounge chairs, enjoy water sports, or take a refreshing swim in the crystal-clear waters. Additionally, Fairmont Royal Pavilion has a swimming pool surrounded by lush tropical gardens, providing a tranquil setting for relaxation.

Spa and Wellness: The resort features a spa where guests can indulge in rejuvenating treatments, massages, and wellness therapies. The spa offers a range of services designed to promote relaxation and well-being. Guests can also take advantage of the fitness centre for their workout routines.

Concierge Services: Fairmont Royal Pavilion provides concierge services to assist guests with various needs, such as arranging excursions, making restaurant reservations, and organizing transportation. The concierge can provide recommendations on local attractions, activities, and cultural experiences.

To get to Fairmont Royal Pavilion, you can fly into Grantley Adams International Airport (BGI) in Barbados. From the airport, you have several transportation options:

Private Transfer: The resort can arrange for a private transfer service to pick you up from the airport and take you directly to the property. This option offers convenience and personalized service.

Taxi: Taxis are readily available at the airport, and you can take one to Fairmont Royal Pavilion. It's advisable to confirm the fare with the driver before getting into the taxi.
Rental Car: If you prefer more flexibility and independence, you can rent a car at the airport and drive to the resort. Barbados has well-maintained roads, and driving is on the left side.

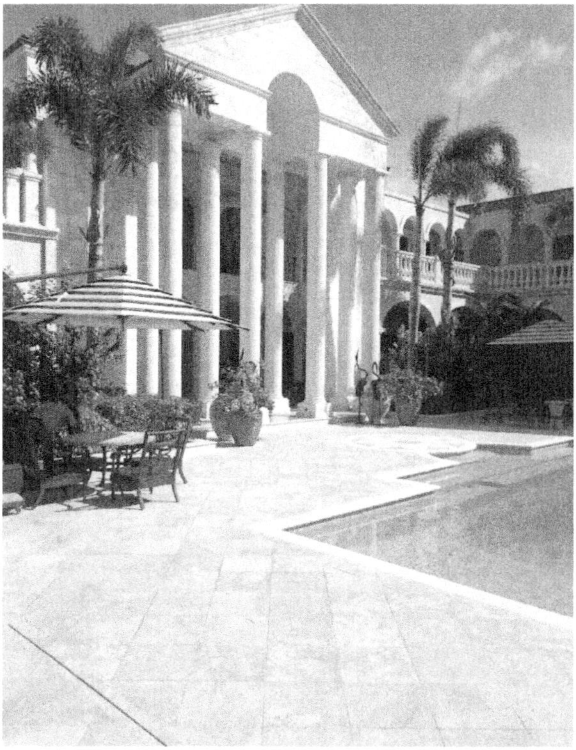

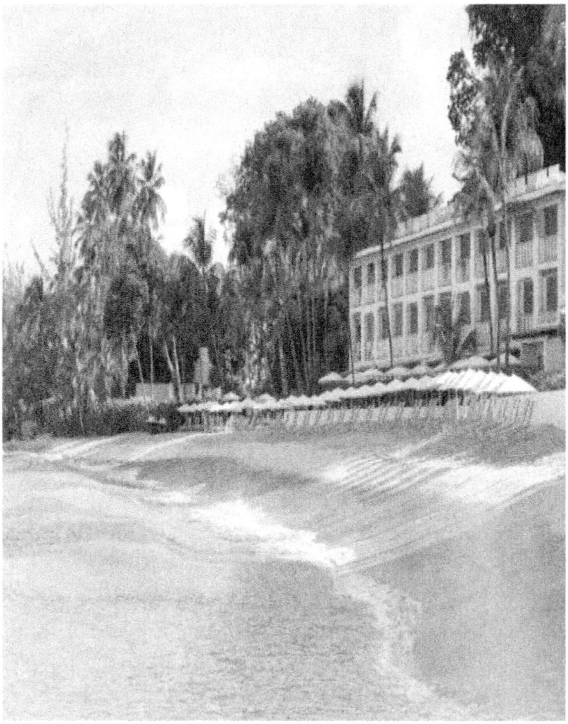

Map and direction from Grantley Adams International Airport (BGI) to Fairmont Royal Pavilion

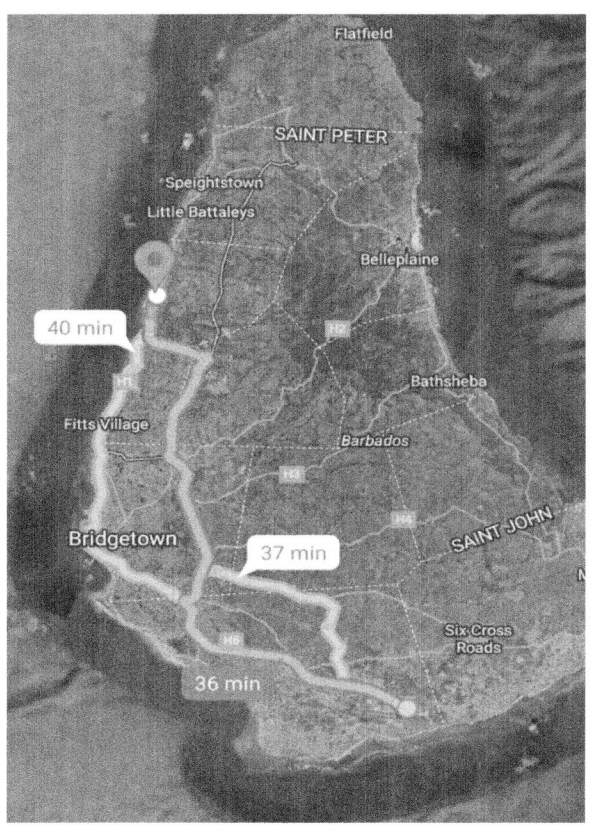

Granted ley Adams International Airport (BGI) to Fairmont Royal Pavilion

36 min (29 km)
Fastest route now due to traffic conditions

Steps

◉ Grantley Adams International Airport

↑ Head west on Airport Access Rd toward S Ramp
400 m

↱ Turn right toward Tom Adams Hwy
50 m

↰ Turn left onto Tom Adams Hwy
1.8 km

⤻ At the roundabout, take the 1st exit and stay on Tom Adams Hwy
30 m

⤴ Exit the roundabout onto Tom Adams Hwy
2.6 km

⤴ At the roundabout, take the 1st exit and stay on Tom Adams Hwy
20 m

Step 1

↱ Exit the roundabout onto Tom Adams Hwy

   3.1 km

↻ At the roundabout, take the 2nd exit and stay on Tom Adams Hwy

   60 m

↱ Exit the roundabout onto Tom Adams Hwy

   1.2 km

↻ At the roundabout, take the 2nd exit onto Errol Barrow Hwy

   90 m

↱ Exit the roundabout onto Errol Barrow Hwy

   1.6 km

↻ At the roundabout, take the 2nd exit and stay on Errol Barrow Hwy

   30 m

↱ Exit the roundabout onto Errol Barrow Hwy

   800 m

⮎ Sharp right to stay on Errol Barrow Hwy

Step 2

- Keep right to stay on Errol Barrow Hwy

  80 m

- At the roundabout, take the 1st exit and stay on Errol Barrow Hwy

  30 m

- Exit the roundabout onto Errol Barrow Hwy

  1.1 km

- At the roundabout, take the 2nd exit and stay on Errol Barrow Hwy

  60 m

- Exit the roundabout onto Errol Barrow Hwy

  1.0 km

- At the roundabout, take the 2nd exit and stay on Errol Barrow Hwy

  30 m

- Exit the roundabout onto Errol Barrow Hwy

  1.9 km

- At the roundabout, take the 1st exit and stay on Errol Barrow Hwy

Step 3

- Exit the roundabout onto Errol Barrow Hwy

    2.2 km

- At the roundabout, take the 2nd exit and stay on Errol Barrow Hwy

    60 m

- Exit the roundabout onto Errol Barrow Hwy

    350 m

- At the roundabout, take the 3rd exit onto Hwy 2A/Ronald Mapp Hwy

    90 m

- Exit the roundabout onto Hwy 2A/Ronald Mapp Hwy

    1.3 km

- At the roundabout, take the 2nd exit and stay on Hwy 2A/Ronald Mapp Hwy

    50 m

- Exit the roundabout onto Hwy 2A/Ronald Mapp Hwy

    800 m

Step 4

- At the roundabout, take the 1st exit and stay on Hwy 2A/Ronald Mapp Hwy

    3.0 km

- At the roundabout, take the 1st exit onto Hwy 1A/Sea View

    30 m

- Exit the roundabout onto Hwy 1A/Sea View

    2.9 km

- Turn right onto Hwy 1

    1.8 km

- Fairmont Royal Pavilion
  Highway 1

Final step

Coral Reef Club: Found on the west coast in the parish of St. James, the address is Holetown, St. James.

Coral Reef Club is an elegant and family-owned luxury resort located in St. James Parish on the West Coast of Barbados. The resort offers a range of services and amenities to provide guests with a tranquil and personalized experience. **Here are some of the services typically offered by Coral Reef Club:**

Accommodations: The resort features spacious and beautifully appointed rooms, suites, and cottages set amidst lush tropical gardens. The accommodations are designed to provide comfort and privacy, with features like private patios or balconies, en-suite bathrooms, and luxurious furnishings.

Dining: Coral Reef Club offers exquisite dining options, including a beachfront restaurant and an open-air terrace. Guests can enjoy a variety of culinary delights, from international dishes to traditional Barbadian cuisine. The resort emphasizes fresh, locally sourced ingredients and personalized service.

Beach and Pools: The resort provides direct access to a pristine white sandy beach, where guests can relax on lounge chairs, soak up the sun, and swim in the turquoise waters. Coral Reef Club also features a swimming pool surrounded by tropical gardens, providing a serene atmosphere for relaxation.

Spa and Wellness: The resort offers a tranquil spa with a range of rejuvenating treatments, massages, and wellness therapies. Guests can indulge in pampering experiences and take advantage of the spa's serene ambience. The resort also provides yoga classes and a fitness centre for those seeking active pursuits.

Activities and Excursions: Coral Reef Club offers various activities and excursions to explore the beauty of Barbados. Guests can enjoy water sports such as snorkelling, kayaking, and paddleboarding. The resort can also arrange off-site adventures, including island tours, catamaran cruises, and visits to local attractions.

To get to Coral Reef Club, you can fly into Grantley Adams International Airport (BGI) in Barbados. From the airport, you have several transportation options:

Private Transfer: The resort can arrange for a private transfer service to pick you up from the airport and take you directly to Coral Reef Club. This option offers convenience and personalized service.

Taxi: Taxis are readily available at the airport, and you can take one to the resort. It's advisable to confirm the fare with the driver before getting into the taxi.

Rental Car: If you prefer more flexibility and independence, you can rent a car at the airport and drive to Coral Reef Club. Barbados has well-maintained roads, and driving is on the left side.

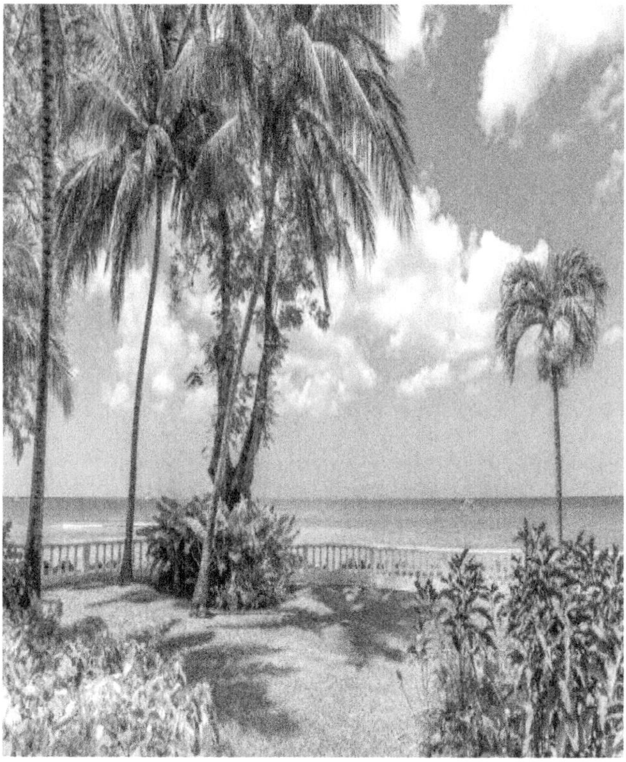

View from room

The spa
Map and directions from Grantley Adams
International Airport (BGI) to Coral Reef Club

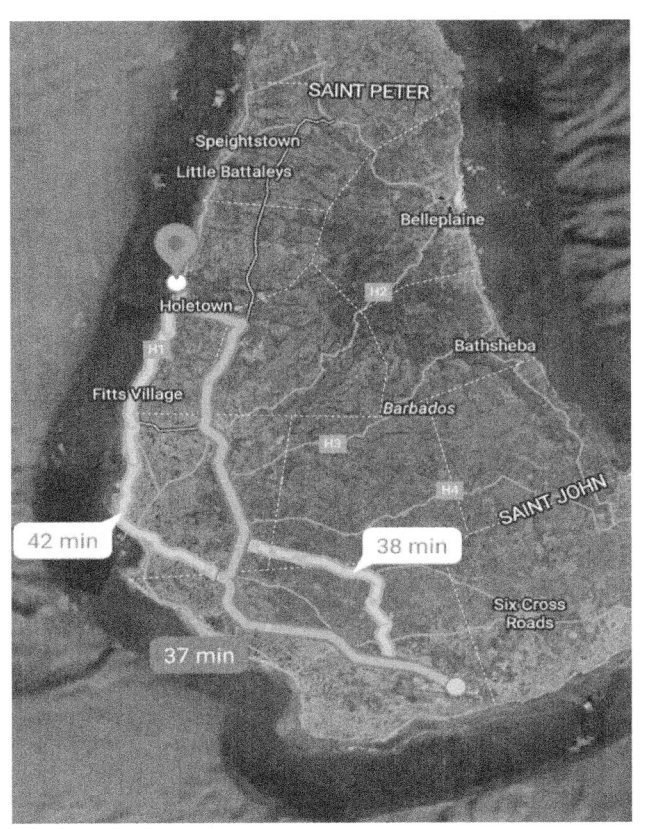

Grantley Adams International Airport (BGI) to Coral Reef Club

37 min ↟ (28 km)

Fastest route now due to traffic conditions, but it's getting worse

Steps

⊙ Grantley Adams International Airport

↑ Head west on Airport Access Rd toward S Ramp

400 m

↱ Turn right toward Tom Adams Hwy

50 m

↰ Turn left onto Tom Adams Hwy

1.8 km

↳ At the roundabout, take the 1st exit and stay on Tom Adams Hwy

30 m

↥ Exit the roundabout onto Tom Adams Hwy

2.6 km

↱ At the roundabout, take the 1st exit and stay on Tom Adams Hwy

Step 1

↗ Exit the roundabout onto Tom Adams Hwy

3.1 km

↻ At the roundabout, take the 2nd exit and stay on Tom Adams Hwy

60 m

↗ Exit the roundabout onto Tom Adams Hwy

1.2 km

↻ At the roundabout, take the 2nd exit onto Errol Barrow Hwy

90 m

↗ Exit the roundabout onto Errol Barrow Hwy

1.6 km

↻ At the roundabout, take the 2nd exit and stay on Errol Barrow Hwy

30 m

↗ Exit the roundabout onto Errol Barrow Hwy

800 m

↱ Sharp right to stay on Errol Barrow Hwy

Step 2

Keep right to stay on Errol Barrow Hwy

80 m

At the roundabout, take the 1st exit and stay on Errol Barrow Hwy

30 m

Exit the roundabout onto Errol Barrow Hwy

1.1 km

At the roundabout, take the 2nd exit and stay on Errol Barrow Hwy

60 m

Exit the roundabout onto Errol Barrow Hwy

1.0 km

At the roundabout, take the 2nd exit and stay on Errol Barrow Hwy

30 m

Exit the roundabout onto Errol Barrow Hwy

1.9 km

Step 3

↻ At the roundabout, take the 1st exit and stay on Errol Barrow Hwy

50 m

↗ Exit the roundabout onto Errol Barrow Hwy

2.2 km

↻ At the roundabout, take the 2nd exit and stay on Errol Barrow Hwy

60 m

↗ Exit the roundabout onto Errol Barrow Hwy

350 m

↻→ At the roundabout, take the 3rd exit onto Hwy 2A/Ronald Mapp Hwy

90 m

↗ Exit the roundabout onto Hwy 2A/Ronald Mapp Hwy

1.3 km

↻ At the roundabout, take the 2nd exit and stay on Hwy 2A/Ronald Mapp Hwy

50 m

Step 4

↱ Exit the roundabout onto Hwy 2A/Ronald Mapp Hwy

800 m

⇢ At the roundabout, take the 1st exit and stay on Hwy 2A/Ronald Mapp Hwy

3.0 km

↰ At the roundabout, take the 1st exit onto Hwy 1A/Sea View

30 m

↱ Exit the roundabout onto Hwy 1A/Sea View

2.9 km

↪ Turn right onto Hwy 1

750 m

↩ Turn left

190 m

⊙ Coral Reef Club
Porters Folkstone St. James

Last step

Hilton Barbados Resort: Positioned in Needhams Point, St. Michael.

Hilton Barbados Resort is a well-known and upscale hotel located in Needhams Point, Bridgetown, Barbados. The resort offers a range of services and amenities to ensure a comfortable and enjoyable stay for guests.

Here are some of the services typically offered by Hilton Barbados Resort:

Accommodations: The resort features spacious and stylishly appointed guest rooms and suites, many of which offer stunning views of the Caribbean Sea. The accommodations are equipped with modern amenities, including flat-screen TVs, mini-fridges, and comfortable bedding.

Dining: Hilton Barbados Resort offers several dining options, including a beachfront restaurant, a poolside bar, and a casual café. Guests can savour a variety of culinary delights, including international cuisine and local Barbadian specialities. The resort's restaurants often provide a relaxed and enjoyable dining experience.

Beach and Pools: The resort provides direct access to a beautiful beach where guests can lounge on sunbeds, soak up the sun, and swim in the clear waters. Hilton Barbados Resort also features multiple swimming pools, including an infinity pool overlooking the ocean, offering a refreshing place to relax and cool off.

Spa and Wellness: The resort offers a spa and fitness centre where guests can indulge in a range of treatments, massages, and wellness services. The spa facilities often include relaxation areas, steam rooms, and saunas. Guests can also enjoy the fitness centre with modern equipment for their workout routines.

Meetings and Events: Hilton Barbados Resort provides versatile meeting and event spaces for conferences, weddings, and other special occasions. The resort offers professional event planning services, state-of-the-art audiovisual equipment, and catering options to ensure successful and memorable gatherings.

To get to Hilton Barbados Resort, you can fly into Grantley Adams International Airport (BGI) in Barbados. From the airport, you have several transportation options:

Taxi: Taxis are readily available at the airport, and you can take one to Hilton Barbados Resort. The resort is approximately 20 minutes away from the airport. It's advisable to confirm the fare with the driver before getting into the taxi.

Rental Car: If you prefer more flexibility and independence, you can rent a car at the airport and drive to the resort. Barbados has well-maintained roads, and driving is on the left side. The resort offers parking facilities for guests.

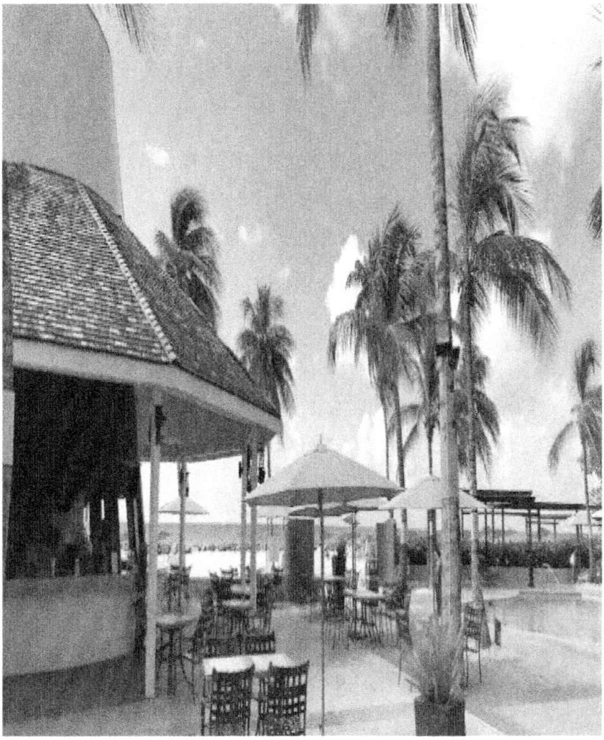

Map and directions from Grantley Adams International Airport (BGI) to Hilton Barbados Resort

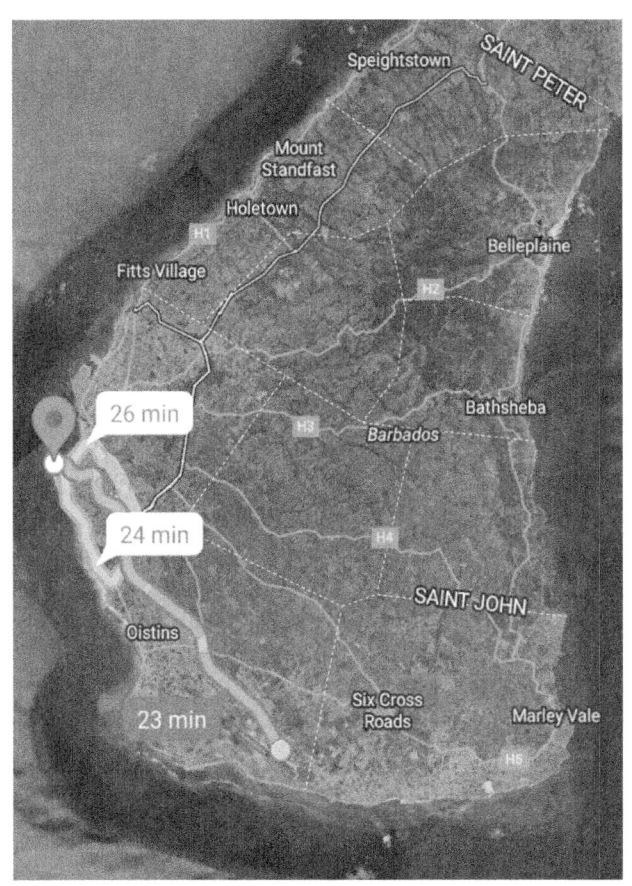

Grantley Adams International Airport (BGI) to Hilton Barbados Resort

23 min (16 km)

Fastest route now due to traffic conditions

Steps

⊙ Grantley Adams International Airport

↑ Head west on Airport Access Rd toward S Ramp

400 m

↱ Turn right toward Tom Adams Hwy

50 m

↰ Turn left onto Tom Adams Hwy

1.8 km

⤺ At the roundabout, take the 1st exit and stay on Tom Adams Hwy

30 m

⤴ Exit the roundabout onto Tom Adams Hwy

2.6 km

⤴ At the roundabout, take the 1st exit and stay on Tom Adams Hwy

20 m

Step 1

Exit the roundabout onto Tom Adams Hwy

3.1 km

At the roundabout, take the 2nd exit and stay on Tom Adams Hwy

60 m

Exit the roundabout onto Tom Adams Hwy

1.2 km

At the roundabout, take the 2nd exit onto Errol Barrow Hwy

90 m

Exit the roundabout onto Errol Barrow Hwy

1.6 km

At the roundabout, take the 1st exit onto Rendezvous Hill

20 m

Exit the roundabout onto Rendezvous Hill

160 m

Turn right onto Forde's Rd

Step 2

← Turn left at Reece Road
  1.1 km

← Turn left onto Dalkeith Road
  550 m

→ Turn right onto Garrison Rd
  450 m

↑ Continue straight onto Bush Hill
  140 m

→ Turn right onto Hwy 7
  80 m

← Turn left onto Aquatic Gap
  400 m

← Turn left to stay on Aquatic Gap
  200 m

📍 Hilton Barbados Resort
  Needham's Point
  ⓘ Destination will be on the left

Final step
Villas and Vacation Rentals:
Port Ferdinand Marina & Luxury Residences: Situated in Six Men's, St. Peter.

Port Ferdinand Marina & Luxury Residences

Port Ferdinand Marina & Luxury Residences

Royal Westmoreland: Located in Royal Westmoreland, St. James.

Royal Westmoreland

Royal Westmoreland
Saint Peter's Bay Luxury Resort & Residences: Found in Road View, St. Peter.

Saint Peter's Bay Luxury Resort & Residences

Saint Peter's Bay Luxury Resort & Residences

Mullins Grove: Situated in Mullins Terrace, St. Peter.

Mullins Grove

Waves Hotel & Spa by Elegant Hotels: Positioned in Prospect, St. James.

Waves Hotel & Spa by Elegant Hotels

Waves Hotel & Spa by Elegant Hotels

Outdoor Activities in Barbados:
Barbados offers a variety of outdoor activities for visitors to enjoy.
Here are some popular activities and their locations:
Beaches:
Crane Beach: Located on the southeast coast in The Crane, St. Philip.
Accra Beach: Found in Rockley, Christ Church.
Mullins Beach: Situated in Mullins, St. Peter.
Bathsheba Beach: Positioned in Bathsheba, St. Joseph.
Miami Beach: Located in Enterprise, Christ Church.
Snorkelling and Diving:
Carlisle Bay Marine Park: Found in Bridgetown, St. Michael.

Folkestone Marine Park: Located in Holetown, St. James.
Surfing:
Soup Bowl: Situated in Bathsheba, St. Joseph.
Freights Bay: Found in Enterprise, Christ Church.
Hiking and Nature:
Harrison's Cave: Located in Welchman Hall, St. Thomas.
Welchman Hall Gully: Found in Welchman Hall, St. Thomas.
Andromeda Botanic Gardens: Positioned in Bathsheba, St. Joseph .h

Itinerary options to explore Barbados based on your desired length of stay

Here are some itinerary options for exploring Barbados like a local, ranging from 3 days to 3 weeks:
3-Day Itinerary:
Day 1:
- Start your day with a visit to Bridgetown, the capital city. Explore historic sites like the Parliament Buildings, National Heroes Square, and the Nidhe Israel Synagogue.

**Parliament Buildings Bridgetown
Address: 39WP+W9H, Rickett St, Bridgetown, Barbados**

National Heroes Square
Address: 39WP+MCC, Bridgetown, Barbados

Nidhe Israel Synagogue
Address: Synagogue Ln, Bridgetown, Barbados
- Head to Carlisle Bay for some beach time. Relax on the white sands, go snorkelling or diving to explore the shipwrecks, or enjoy water sports activities.

Carlisle Bay

Carlisle Bay
- In the evening, visit Oistins Fish Fry, a local hotspot for delicious seafood and live music.

Day 2:
- Spend the day exploring the eastern coast of Barbados. Start at Bathsheba, known for its dramatic rock formations and pounding surf. Enjoy a stroll along the beach.

Bathsheba
- Visit the Andromeda Botanic Gardens, a beautiful tropical garden with a wide variety of plants and flowers.

Andromeda Botanic Gardens

Andromeda Botanic Gardens

Andromeda Botanic Gardens

Address: Off Highway 3, Bathsheba, Barbados
- Head to St. Nicholas Abbey, a historic plantation house where you can learn about the island's sugar cane industry and sample some rum.

St. Nicholas Abbey

Address: Cherry Tree Hill St. Peter, BB26007, Barbados

Day 3:
- Take a day trip to the Animal Flower Cave on the northern tip of the island. Explore the cave, enjoy panoramic views of the Atlantic Ocean, and take a dip in the natural rock pools.

Animal Flower Cave

Animal Flower Cave

Address: North Point, Conneltown, Barbados
- Visit Holetown, a charming town with a rich history. Explore the Chattel Village for local crafts and souvenirs, and stroll along the picturesque boardwalk.

5-Day Itinerary:
Day 4:
- Explore the west coast of Barbados, also known as the Platinum Coast. Visit Paynes Bay Beach for swimming and sunbathing.
- Take a catamaran cruise to swim with sea turtles and snorkel over coral reefs.
- Visit the Mount Gay Rum Distillery to learn about the island's rum-making heritage and enjoy a tasting session.

Day 5:
- Spend the day at Harrison's Cave, a natural wonder with magnificent underground caverns. Take a tram tour and marvel at the stalactites, stalagmites, and underground streams.
- Visit the Barbados Museum & Historical Society to learn about the island's history and culture.
- Enjoy a traditional Bajan meal at one of the local restaurants.

7-Day Itinerary:
Day 6:
- Explore the rugged Atlantic coast of Barbados. Visit the cliffs at Cove Bay and explore the nearby Animal Flower Cave.
- Take a surfing lesson at Bathsheba or try boogie boarding along the coast.
- Visit the Barbados Wildlife Reserve to see green monkeys, tortoises, and other native animals.

Day 7:
- Spend the day in the south of the island. Visit the historic Garrison area, a UNESCO World Heritage Site, and explore the Barbados Museum and George Washington House.
- Relax at Accra Beach, known for its golden sand and clear waters.
- Enjoy a sunset dinner at one of the beachfront restaurants in St. Lawrence Gap.

2-Week Itinerary:
Day 8-13:
- Spend a few days exploring Barbados' lesser-known attractions. Visit the rugged east coast and explore secluded beaches like Bottom Bay and Crane Beach.
- Take a day trip to the nearby island of Martinique or St. Lucia for a change of scenery.
- Visit the Welchman Hall Gully, a tropical forest with winding paths and exotic plants.
- Explore the historic plantation houses in the countryside, such as Sunbury Plantation House and St. Nicholas Abbey.

Day 14:
- Relax and unwind at one of the island's luxury resorts. Enjoy the amenities, indulge in spa treatments, and take advantage of the beautiful beaches.

3-Week Itinerary:
Days 15-21:
- Spend the final week immersing yourself in local culture. Attend a cricket match at the Kensington Oval, a historic cricket ground in Bridgetown.

- Visit local markets like Cheapside Market and Brighton Farmers Market to experience the vibrant atmosphere and sample fresh produce.
- Attend a traditional Bajan music or dance performance, such as a steel pan concert or a folk dancing show.
- Explore the countryside further by taking scenic drives through the scenic landscapes and stopping at charming villages along the way.
- Participate in a cooking or cocktail-making class to learn how to prepare authentic Bajan dishes and drinks.
- Spend time volunteering with a local organization or participating in a community project to give back to the community and learn more about the island's social initiatives.

These itineraries offer a mix of cultural, historical, natural, and culinary experiences, allowing you to immerse yourself in the local lifestyle and discover the hidden gems of Barbados. Remember to check local travel guidelines, and attractions' opening hours, and make any necessary reservations in advance to ensure a smooth and enjoyable trip.

A day trip in Barbados

You're in for something special if you're thinking of taking a day trip to Barbados! This island in the Caribbean is well-known for its breathtaking beaches, fascinating past, and lively culture.

The following is a proposed route for a special day excursion in Barbados:

Morning:

Visit Harrison's Cave first thing in the morning. With its stunning stalactites and stalagmites, this limestone cave is a natural treasure. Explore the cave's beautiful structures and discover its geological significance by taking a guided tram tour.

After visiting the cave, travel to Bathsheba on Barbados' east coast. This seaside community is renowned for its untamed beauty, stunning rock formations, and crashing waves. Take in the beautiful environment as you go along the beach and get some fantastic images.

Make your way to the neighbouring Andromeda Botanic Gardens from Bathsheba. Many different exotic plants and flowers can be found in this tropical paradise. Enjoy the tranquilly of the surroundings while taking a stroll through the garden's winding walkways and admiring the vibrant blooms.

Afternoon:

It's time to unwind on the beach! Visit Carlisle Bay or Accra Beach, two of Barbados' well-known west coast beaches. Enjoy some time in the sun, a dip in the pristine waters, and some water sports like snorkelling or paddleboarding.

Try some Bajan cuisine for lunch. Try foods like spicy jerk chicken, cou-cou (a cornmeal and okra dish), macaroni pie, and flying fish. You may sample the flavours of Barbados at many coastal eateries and food stands.

Drive a short distance to Bridgetown, Barbados's capital, after lunch. Discover the UNESCO World Heritage Site known as the Garrison, a historic district. Visit sites including St. Ann's Fort, George Washington House, and the Barbados Museum & Historical Society.

Evening:

As the day comes to an end, stop by Oistins Fish Fry for a fun experience. The fishing community of Oistins hosts this well-liked Friday night event, but it's also open on other evenings. Enjoy live music, delicious seafood, and a fun atmosphere.

Take a leisurely sunset cruise to cap off your day. On catamaran cruises, you may take in breath-taking scenery, sip rum punch, and even go swimming with turtles. It's the ideal way to unwind and take in Barbados' stunning shoreline.

Here are the directions to each of the mentioned places in Barbados, assuming you have a car or are willing to trek:

Harrison's Cave:

Harrison's Cave

Harrison's Cave
Location: Welchman Hall, St. Thomas
Directions: From Bridgetown, take Highway 2 heading northeast. Continue on Highway 2 until you reach Welchman Hall. Look for signs indicating Harrison's Cave. The cave is easily accessible by car, and there is ample parking available.
Bathsheba:

Bathsheba
Location: East coast of Barbados
Directions: From Harrison's Cave, head east on Highway 2 until you reach the coast. Turn left (north) on Highway 3, and follow the signs to Bathsheba. The drive offers scenic views, and Bathsheba is well-marked along the way.
Andromeda Botanic Gardens:

Andromeda Botanic Gardens
Location: Foster Hall, St. Joseph
Directions: From Bathsheba, head south on Highway 3. Continue until you reach Foster Hall. Look for signs pointing to Andromeda Botanic Gardens. The gardens are easily accessible by car, and parking is available on-site.
Carlisle Bay or Accra Beach:

Accra Beach
Location: South or southwestern coast of Barbados
Directions to Carlisle Bay: From Andromeda Botanic Gardens, take Highway 3 heading south. Continue on Highway 3 until you reach Bridgetown. Carlisle Bay is located just south of Bridgetown, and there are parking facilities available.
Directions to Accra Beach: From Andromeda Botanic Gardens, head south on Highway 3. Continue on Highway 3 until you reach Rockley. Turn right onto Highway 7 and follow it until you reach Accra Beach. Parking is available near the beach.
Bridgetown:
Location: Southwest coast of Barbados
Directions: From either Carlisle Bay or Accra Beach, take Highway 7 heading south. Continue on Highway 7 until you reach Bridgetown. The city has various parking lots

and street parking options available. Once in Bridgetown, follow signs to specific attractions like the Garrison or George Washington House.

Oistins Fish Fry:

Oistins Fish market

Location: Oistins, Christ Church
Directions: From Bridgetown, take Highway 7 heading southeast. Continue on Highway 7 until you reach Oistins. Signs for Oistins Fish Fry are prominent in the area, and parking is available near the Oistins Fish Market.

Here are the approximate opening hours for the mentioned attractions in Barbados:

Harrison's Cave:
Opening Hours: Daily from 9:00 AM to 3:45 PM
Guided tram tours depart every 45 minutes

Andromeda Botanic Gardens:
Opening Hours: Monday to Saturday from 9:00 AM to 4:30 PM
Note: The gardens are closed on Sundays and public holidays.

Barbados Museum & Historical Society:

Opening Hours: Monday to Saturday from 9:00 AM to 5:00 PM

Note: The museum is closed on Sundays and public holidays.

George Washington House:

Opening Hours: Monday to Saturday from 9:00 AM to 4:30 PM

Note: The house is closed on Sundays and public holidays.

Please note that opening hours can sometimes vary, so it's a good idea to check the specific attraction's website or contact them directly for the most up-to-date information. Additionally, some attractions may require a booking or have limited availability, so it's advisable to plan accordingly.

Museums and galleries to visit in Barbados

Barbados is renowned for its thriving art scene and rich cultural heritage.

You can visit the following galleries and museums while visiting Barbados:

Barbados Museum and Historical Society:

Barbados Museum and Historical Society
The Barbados Museum, which is situated in Bridgetown, the nation's capital, provides a thorough look into the island's past. A former British military jail now serves as the museum, which has displays on Barbadian antiquity, slavery, colonialism, and natural history.
Arlington House Museum:

Arlington House Museum

Arlington House, a restored 18th-century structure near Speightstown, offers a window into the island's colonial past. The museum features interactive exhibits, audio-visual shows, and exhibits about Barbados' history and culture.

George Washington House:

George Washington House
The first American president, George Washington, slept in this old mansion in Bridgetown when he came to Barbados in 1751. The museum gives tours and displays about Barbados' colonial past and Washington's time there.

Welchman Hall Gully:

Welchman Hall Gully
Welchman Hall Gully is a botanical reserve with a varied array of tropical plants and trees, yet it is not a typical museum or gallery. You can join a guided trip to see the alluring gully and discover more about Barbados's flora and animals.

Gallery of Caribbean Art:

Gallery of Caribbean Art
The Gallery of Caribbean Art, which is in Speightstown, features both modern and traditional Caribbean art. The gallery offers a glimpse into the thriving Caribbean art scene by displaying works by local and regional artists in the forms of paintings, sculptures, ceramics, and mixed media.
Frank Collymore Hall:

Frank Collymore Hall
The Frank Collymore Hall is a performing arts venue in Bridgetown that offers a variety of cultural activities, such as art exhibitions, musical performances, and theatrical productions. If you want to know if there will be any exhibitions or performances during your visit, check their schedule.
Chalky Mount Potteries:
Chalky Mount Potteries is a worthwhile stop for anyone interested in traditional pottery even though it's not a museum. You can see local artisans employing age-old techniques to create lovely clay ceramics at St. Andrew Parish. You might even get the chance to buy one-of-a-kind handmade items.
Barbados National Gallery:
The Barbados National Gallery, which is in Bridgetown, is devoted to displaying the creations of Barbadian and Caribbean artists. A wide variety of modern and traditional

works of art, including paintings, sculptures, photographs, and mixed media pieces, are on display in the gallery.
Harrison's Cave:

Harrison's Cave

Harrison's Cave is a well-known tourist destination in Barbados despite not being a standard museum or gallery. Visitors can explore magnificent limestone caverns, stalactites, and stalagmites in this unique underground adventure. The cave has educational exhibits regarding the history and geological formation of the cave.

Frangipani Art Gallery:
The Frangipani Art Gallery is a modern Caribbean art gallery located in Speightstown. Paintings, sculptures, and mixed-media pieces by renowned and up-and-coming Barbadian and Caribbean artists are on display in the gallery.

Sir Frank Hutson Sugar Museum:

This museum, which is situated in Portvale, St. James Parish, offers information about Barbados' sugar business, which had a huge impact on the history of the island. Visitors can examine exhibits on the effects of the sugar business on Barbadian society, view ancient machinery, and learn about the sugar-producing process.

Arlington Cultural Museum:
The Arlington Cultural Museum in Speightstown is next to Arlington House and focuses on Barbados' rich cultural history. It features relics, images, and hands-on exhibits that illustrate the island's customs, music, dance, and festivals.

Earthworks Pottery:

Earthworks Pottery
Earthworks Pottery is an operating pottery workshop and gallery that is situated in St. Thomas Parish. Visitors may watch local potters create clay ware, browse a variety of handcrafted ceramic items, and even participate in

workshops where they can try their hand at making pottery.

Cricket Legends of Barbados Museum:

Cricket Legends of Barbados Museum

Cricket is a popular sport in Barbados, and the Cricket Legends of Barbados Museum in Bridgetown honours the sport's history on the island. It features artefacts, images, and hands-on exhibits on legendary cricket players from Barbados and the sport's influence on the nation.

Here is the direction by car and by trekking for each of the museums and galleries mention:

Barbados Museum and Historical Society:

By Car: From Bridgetown, head east on Highway 7 (Fontabelle Road) until you reach St. Ann's Garrison. The museum is located on your left.

By Trekking: You can also walk from Bridgetown to the museum by heading east along the main road, passing Independence Square and continuing on Highway 7 until you reach St. Ann's Garrison.

Arlington House Museum:

By Car: From Bridgetown, take Highway 1 (Spring Garden Highway) heading north. Continue on Highway 1 until you reach Speightstown. Arlington House is located in the town centre.

By Trekking: If you prefer trekking, you can walk along Highway 1 from Bridgetown to Speightstown. It's a scenic coastal route, but it can be a long walk, so plan accordingly.

George Washington House:

By Car: From Bridgetown, take Bay Street heading south until you reach the St. Ann's Garrison area. The George Washington House is located within the Garrison Historic Area.

By Trekking: You can walk from Bridgetown to the George Washington House by heading south along Bay Street until you reach the St. Ann's Garrison area. It's a relatively short walk from the city centre.

Welchman Hall Gully:

By Car: From Bridgetown, take Highway 2B heading northeast towards St. Thomas. Look for signs directing you to Welchman Hall Gully.

By Trekking: If you enjoy trekking, you can hike from Bridgetown to Welchman Hall Gully by following Highway 2B. It's a long trek, so make sure you are prepared with proper footwear and supplies.

Please note that it's essential to plan your trekking routes carefully, consider weather conditions, and ensure your safety during the journey.

Gallery of Caribbean Art:

By Car: From Bridgetown, take Highway 1 (Spring Garden Highway) heading north. Continue on Highway 1 until you reach Speightstown. The gallery is located in the town centre.

By Trekking: You can walk along Highway 1 from Bridgetown to Speightstown, enjoying the coastal views along the way. The gallery is located in the centre of Speightstown.

Frank Collymore Hall:

By Car: From Bridgetown, head south along Bay Street until you reach Hincks Street. Turn left onto Hincks Street, and the Frank Collymore Hall will be on your right.

By Trekking: You can walk from Bridgetown to Frank Collymore Hall by heading south along Bay Street until you reach Hincks Street. It's a relatively short walk from the city centre.

Chalky Mount Potteries:

By Car: Chalky Mount Potteries is located in St. Andrew Parish. From Bridgetown, take Highway 2A heading north and continue until you reach Chalky Mount. Look for signs indicating the pottery.

By Trekking: Trekking to Chalky Mount Potteries is not recommended, as it's located in a rural area. It's best to reach there by car or taxi.

Barbados National Gallery:

By Car: From Bridgetown, head south along Bay Street until you reach the Garrison Savannah area. The Barbados National Gallery is located near Savannah, and you can find parking nearby.

By Trekking: You can walk from Bridgetown to the Barbados National Gallery by heading south along Bay Street until you reach the Garrison Savannah. It's a moderate walk from the city centre.

Harrison's Cave:

By Car: Harrison's Cave is located in the central part of the island. From Bridgetown, you can take Highway 3 (Ronald Mapp Highway) heading northeast until you reach the cave entrance. Follow the signs along the way.

By Trekking: Trekking to Harrison's Cave is not recommended, as it's quite a distance from Bridgetown and mostly accessible by road.

Frangipani Art Gallery:

By Car: Frangipani Art Gallery is located in Speightstown. From Bridgetown, take Highway 1 (Spring Garden Highway) heading north. Continue on Highway 1 until you reach Speightstown. The gallery is located in the town centre.

By Trekking: You can walk along Highway 1 from Bridgetown to Speightstown, enjoying the coastal views along the way. The gallery is located in the centre of Speightstown.

Sir Frank Hutson Sugar Museum:

By Car: The Sir Frank Hutson Sugar Museum is located in Portvale, St. James Parish. From Bridgetown, you can take Highway 1 (Spring Garden Highway) heading north. Continue on Highway 1 until you reach Portvale. Look for signs leading to the museum.

By Trekking: Trekking to the Sir Frank Hutson Sugar Museum is not recommended, as it's located inland and best reached by car or taxi.

Arlington Cultural Museum:

By Car: Arlington Cultural Museum is located in Speightstown. From Bridgetown, take Highway 1 (Spring Garden Highway) heading north. Continue on Highway 1 until you reach Speightstown. The museum is located in the town centre.

By Trekking: You can walk along Highway 1 from Bridgetown to Speightstown, enjoying the coastal views along the way. The museum is located in the centre of Speightstown.

Earthworks Pottery:

By Car: Earthworks Pottery is located in St. Thomas Parish. From Bridgetown, take Highway 2B heading northeast towards St. Thomas. Look for signs directing you to Earthworks Pottery.

By Trekking: Trekking to Earthworks Pottery is not recommended, as it's located inland and best reached by car or taxi.

Cricket Legends of Barbados Museum:

By Car: The Cricket Legends of Barbados Museum is located in Bridgetown. From anywhere in Bridgetown, you can easily reach the museum by car or taxi. The exact location will depend on the specific address of the museum, which can be obtained through local sources or online resources.

Festivals and Events

Barbados is renowned for its thriving culture and extensive history, which are highlighted by several annual festivals and events. Even if I can give you details on some well-known festivals and events in Barbados, confirming the most recent details and dates is usually a smart move before making travel arrangements.

The following festivals and events are notable in Barbados:

Crop Over:
Barbados' largest and most well-known celebration, Crop Over, lasts for several weeks from June to August. It began as a way to mark the end of the sugar cane harvest but has now grown into a vibrant extravaganza of parades, music, dancing, and cultural activities. In the Grand Kadooment procession, which marks the festival's conclusion, revellers dance through Bridgetown's streets while wearing ornate costumes.

Holetown Festival:
This celebration honours the first settlers' arrival in Holetown, Barbados, in 1627. The festival, which is held in February, includes several events like street fairs, musical performances, historical reenactments, and a large parade. The festival showcases Barbados' regional customs, culture, and legacy.

Barbados Reggae Festival:
Fans of reggae music shouldn't miss the Barbados Reggae Festival, which typically takes place in April or May. With activities including beach parties, concerts, and the well-known Reggae Beach Party, the festival has a lineup of regional and international reggae musicians.

Oistins Fish Festival:
The Oistins Fish Festival honours Barbados' renowned seafood industry and the island's fishing people. The celebration, which takes place during Easter weekend in the fishing community of Oistins, includes fish markets, culinary contests, live music, cultural performances, and, of course, a lot of delectable seafood.

Holders Season:
Holders Season is an annual performing arts festival that mixes music, theatre, and storytelling. It is held on the breathtaking grounds of Holders House. The festival,

which typically takes place in March or April and features renowned performers from around the world, offers a distinctive cultural experience.

Barbados Food and Rum Festival:
The Barbados Food and Rum Festival, which celebrates the island's culinary offerings and rum culture, is a must-attend event for foodies. The event, which is typically held in October, offers a variety of gourmet experiences, including food tastings, cooking demos, mixology classes, and more.

Barbados Jazz Festival:
The annual Barbados Jazz Festival, which brings together local and international jazz musicians, will be enjoyed by jazz fans. The festival, which normally happens in January, includes several concerts and shows at several locations throughout the island.

Barbados Independent Film Festival:
The Barbados Independent Film Festival offers a wide variety of independent films from all around the world for movie fans to enjoy. The festival offers the chance to see screenings, participate in workshops and panel discussions, and talk to filmmakers. The festival's dates could change, so it's best to check the official website for the most recent details.

Holders Polo Season:
The Holders Polo Season, which runs from January to April, features a fun mix of sports and socialising. In the magnificent grounds of Holders House, guests may take in picnics, social gatherings, and live music while watching thrilling polo matches.

Barbados Sailing Week:
During Barbados Sailing Week, sailors can take part in the thrilling races or observe them. This competition, which

takes place in January, draws sailors from all over the world to compete in several classes. Additionally, there are events and activities on the beach to enjoy every day of the week.

Barbados Visual Arts Festival:
The annual Barbados Visual Arts Festival, which celebrates the visual arts on the island, will be enjoyed by art enthusiasts. The festival, which usually takes place in November, offers the opportunity to interact with both local and foreign artists through exhibitions, workshops, and art talks.

Market in Bridgetown:
Bridgetown Market is a bustling street market that takes place in the nation's capital during the summer. It offers a sample of the local culture and entertainment through food stalls, craft merchants, live music, cultural acts, and a lively atmosphere.

Here's a brief guide on how to locate some of the festivals and events in Barbados, whether by car or trekking:

Crop Over: Crop Over events take place throughout Barbados, but the main activities and the Grand Kadooment parade are centred in Bridgetown. Bridgetown is easily accessible by car or public transportation. You can rent a car and use GPS or follow signs to reach Bridgetown. Alternatively, you can take a taxi or use the local bus system to get to the festival venues.

Holetown Festival: Holetown is located on the western coast of Barbados. To reach Holetown by car, you can drive along Highway 1 (West Coast Road). Look for signs indicating Holetown or the festival venues. If you prefer trekking, you can explore the beautiful coastline and walk along the beach from nearby areas.

Barbados Reggae Festival: The Barbados Reggae Festival hosts events at various venues across the island, including beach parties and concerts. The locations may vary each year, so it's best to check the festival's official website or local event listings for specific venue details. You can use a car or taxi to reach the venues, following directions provided or using GPS.

Oistins Fish Festival: Oistins is a fishing village located on the southern coast of Barbados. To reach Oistins by car, you can take Highway 7 (South Coast Road). Look for signs indicating Oistins or the festival grounds. If you prefer trekking, you can explore the coastal areas and walk from nearby towns or beaches.

Holders Season: Holders House, the venue for Holders Season, is situated in St. James parish, near Holetown. You can follow the directions mentioned earlier for the Holetown Festival to reach Holders House. Driving by car or taking a taxi would be the most convenient option for transportation.

Barbados Food and Rum Festival: The Barbados Food and Rum Festival hosts events at various venues across the island. The locations may include hotels, restaurants, and other culinary establishments. You can use a car or taxi to reach the specific venues, following directions provided or using GPS.

Barbados Jazz Festival: The Barbados Jazz Festival events take place at various venues across the island. The locations may include concert halls, outdoor stages, or beachside venues. You can use a car or taxi to reach the specific venues, following directions provided or using GPS. It's a good idea to check the festival's official website or local event listings for the exact locations and transportation details.

Barbados Independent Film Festival: The Barbados Independent Film Festival screenings and events are typically held at different venues, such as theatres or cultural centres. The festival organizers usually provide information about the venues and screening schedules on their official website. You can use a car or taxi to reach the venues, follow directions or use GPS.

Holders Polo Season: Holders Polo Season takes place at the Holders Polo Field, located near Holders House in St. James parish. You can follow the directions mentioned earlier for the Holetown Festival to reach Holders House. From there, it's a short distance to the polo field. Driving by car or taking a taxi would be the most convenient option for transportation.

Barbados Sailing Week: Barbados Sailing Week events are centred around the Carlisle Bay area in Bridgetown and the nearby Barbados Yacht Club. You can use a car or taxi to reach the venues, follow directions or use GPS. Public transportation may also be available in these areas.

Barbados Visual Arts Festival: The Barbados Visual Arts Festival may have exhibitions and events at various locations, such as galleries or cultural centres. The festival organizers usually provide information about the venues and schedules on their official website. You can use a car or taxi to reach the venues, follow directions or use GPS.

Bridgetown Market: Bridgetown Market takes place in the capital city of Bridgetown. You can reach Bridgetown by car, following the main highways or roads that lead to the city. Look for parking facilities near the festival area or follow signs indicating event parking. If you prefer trekking, you can explore the city on foot or use public transportation to reach Bridgetown.

As with any event or festival, it's always a good idea to plan your transportation, check for any road closures or traffic advisories, and consider parking availability or alternatives like using taxis or public transportation.

Outdoor Adventures in Barbados

Barbados, known for its stunning beaches and warm climate, offers a wide range of outdoor adventures for travellers and tourists. Whether you're seeking thrilling water activities, exploring natural wonders, or enjoying the island's diverse landscapes, Barbados has something to offer everyone.

Here are some popular outdoor adventures you can experience in Barbados:

Scuba Diving and Snorkeling: Discover the vibrant underwater world of Barbados by diving or snorkelling in its crystal-clear waters. Explore colourful coral reefs, and ships worshipped encounter a variety of marine life, including tropical fish, sea turtles, and rays.

Surfing and Windsurfing: With its consistent trade winds and excellent surf breaks, Barbados is a popular destination for surfers and windsurfers. Head to the east coast, known as the "Soup Bowl," for world-class waves or try your hand at windsurfing in Silver Sands.

Sailing and Catamaran Cruises: Embark on a sailing adventure along Barbados' coastline or join a catamaran cruise to explore the island's stunning beaches and enjoy snorkelling, swimming with turtles, and a delicious onboard barbecue.

Hiking and Nature Trails: Lace up your hiking boots and explore Barbados' natural beauty. Visit places like Welchman Hall Gully, a tropical forest reserve, or explore Harrison's Cave, an incredible limestone cave system. You can also hike along the rugged coastline, taking in breathtaking views of the Atlantic Ocean.

Wildlife Encounters: Barbados is home to a diverse range of wildlife, including green monkeys, which are native to the island. Visit the Barbados Wildlife Reserve to observe these playful creatures up close, along with other native animals such as tortoises, deer, and agoutis.

Kayaking and Paddleboarding: Rent a kayak or paddleboard and navigate the calm waters along Barbados' coastlines. You can explore secluded bays, paddle through mangrove forests, or venture out to see the picturesque offshore rock formations, like the famous Animal Flower Cave.

Island Safari: Embark on an exhilarating island safari tour, where you'll ride in an open-air jeep and explore the off-the-beaten-path locations of Barbados. Discover hidden gems, and breathtaking viewpoints, and learn about the island's rich history and culture.

Horseback Riding: Experience the beauty of Barbados' landscapes on horseback. Ride along sandy beaches, through lush countryside, and even swim with the horses in the warm Caribbean Sea. It's a unique way to connect with nature and enjoy the island's scenery.

Ziplining: For an adrenaline rush, try ziplining through the treetops in Barbados. Several zipline parks offer thrilling experiences, allowing you to soar above the forest canopy and enjoy panoramic views of the island.

Golfing: Barbados boasts several world-class golf courses, set amidst stunning coastal scenery. Enjoy a round of golf at courses designed by renowned architects while soaking up the island's beauty.

Here's a guide on how to locate and participate in each of the mentioned outdoor adventures in Barbados, whether by car or trekking:

Scuba Diving and Snorkeling:

Locations: Barbados has numerous dive shops and snorkelling spots along its coast. Some popular dive sites include Carlisle Bay Marine Park, Folkestone Marine Park, and the Stavronikita wreck.

Participation: Contact a reputable dive centre or snorkelling operator to arrange a guided trip or rent equipment. They can provide transportation to the dive sites, or you can drive to the designated meeting point.

Surfing and Windsurfing:

Locations: The east coast of Barbados, particularly Bathsheba and the Soup Bowl, is known for its excellent surf breaks. Silver Sands on the south coast is a popular windsurfing spot.

Participation: If you have your equipment, you can drive to the respective surf spots. Alternatively, you can join a surf or windsurfing school that offers lessons, equipment rental, and transportation.

Sailing and Catamaran Cruises:

Locations: Catamaran cruises typically depart from Bridgetown, the capital of Barbados, or popular beaches such as Carlisle Bay and Holetown.

Participation: Book a catamaran cruise with a reputable tour operator. They will provide transportation to the departure point, and the cruise will include snorkelling, swimming, and a barbecue lunch or refreshments.

Hiking and Nature Trails:

Locations: Barbados offers various hiking trails, such as Welchman Hall Gully, Flower Forest, and the rugged east coast. Harrison's Cave has guided tours.

Participation: For self-guided hikes, you can rent a car and drive to the trailheads. Some trails have designated parking areas. For Harrison's Cave, you can drive or take a taxi to the site and join a guided tour.

Wildlife Encounters:

Location: The Barbados Wildlife Reserve is located in the parish of Saint Peter.

Participation: You can drive or take a taxi to the Barbados Wildlife Reserve. The reserve has walking paths that allow you to observe the animals at your own pace.

Kayaking and Paddleboarding:

Locations: You can rent kayaks and paddleboards from various rental operators located at beaches such as Carlisle Bay, Accra Beach, and Miami Beach.

Participation: Drive or take a taxi to the beach where the rental operator is located. They will provide you with the necessary equipment and instructions on kayaking or paddleboarding.

Island Safari:

Locations: Island safari tours usually depart from Bridgetown or other designated pick-up points.

Participation: Book an island safari tour with a reputable operator. They will arrange transportation and pick you up from your hotel or a specified meeting point.

Horseback Riding:

Locations: Horseback riding tours are available in various parts of Barbados, including beaches, countryside, and the east coast.

Participation: Book a horseback riding tour with a reputable operator. They will provide transportation to the starting point of the ride or arrange a pick-up.

Ziplining:

Location: The Barbados zipline parks are located in the parish of Saint Thomas.

Participation: Drive or take a taxi to the zipline park. They will provide all the necessary equipment and guide you through the ziplining experience.

Golfing:

Locations: Barbados offers several golf courses, including Sandy Lane Golf Course, Apes Hill Club, and Royal Westmoreland.

Participation: Contact the golf courses directly to inquire about tee times and availability.

Here are directions on how to get to each location mentioned in Barbados, either by car or trekking:

Scuba Diving and Snorkeling:

Directions: You can drive to these locations by following the main coastal roads. Use a GPS or map for specific directions. Alternatively, you can take a taxi or public transportation to the nearest beach access points.

Surfing and Windsurfing:

Directions: To reach Bathsheba and the Soup Bowl, drive east from Bridgetown along the ABC Highway (Highway 5) and follow signs to Bathsheba. For Silver Sands, drive south from Bridgetown along Highway 7 and follow signs to Silver Sands.

Sailing and Catamaran Cruises:

Directions: Drive to Bridgetown or the designated departure point and follow signs for the specific catamaran cruise company. Taxis are also available and can take you directly to the departure location.

Hiking and Nature Trails:
Directions: To reach Welchman Hall Gully and Flower Forest, drive to their respective locations using a GPS or map for specific directions. For Harrison's Cave, drive to St. Thomas and follow signs to the cave. Taxis are also available for transportation.

Wildlife Encounters:
Directions: Drive north from Bridgetown along Highway 1 and continue until you reach Saint Peter. Look for signs indicating the Barbados Wildlife Reserve. Taxis can also take you directly to the reserve.

Kayaking and Paddleboarding:
Directions: Drive to the respective beaches using a GPS or map. Look for signs indicating the rental operators or beach access points. Taxis can also take you to these locations.

Island Safari:
Directions: Drive to Bridgetown or the specified pick-up location. Follow the instructions provided by the tour operator for the exact meeting point. Taxis are also an option for transportation.

Horseback Riding:
Directions: Follow the directions provided by the horseback riding tour operator for the specific location. They will usually provide detailed instructions on how to reach the starting point. Taxis can also take you directly to the location.

Ziplining:
Directions: Drive to Saint Thomas using a GPS or map. Look for signs indicating the zipline park. Taxis can also take you directly to the park.

Golfing:

Directions: Use a GPS or map to drive to the specific golf course you wish to visit. The courses are located in different areas of Barbados, so follow the directions provided by the respective golf course or contact them directly for specific instructions. Taxis can also take you directly to the golf courses.

Remember to plan your routes, check for any road closures or construction, and allow enough time for transportation. It's also a good idea to have a map or GPS device with you to navigate the island more easily. Enjoy your outdoor adventures in Barbados!

Shopping and Souvenirs in Barbados

Barbados is a stunning Caribbean island that draws a large number of travellers and tourists every year. Barbados has a range of possibilities for shopping and souvenirs to accommodate all interests and preferences.

In Barbados, the following are some well-liked stores and products for shopping and souvenirs:
Bridgetown:

Your shopping expedition should get off to a wonderful start in Barbados' capital city. Numerous shops, boutiques, and duty-free establishments can be found around the city, selling a variety of goods like apparel, jewellery, handicrafts from the area, and more. In Bridgetown, Broad Street is a well-liked shopping district.
Chattel Village:

Chattel Village, a cluster of vividly painted wooden stores offering a selection of regional handicrafts, apparel, jewellery, and souvenirs, is situated in Holetown. The local craftspeople are supported, and it's a terrific place to find unusual goods.

Pelican Craft Centre:

The Pelican Craft Centre in Bridgetown is a paradise for art enthusiasts and souvenir shoppers. You can look around a lot of the stores and stalls here that sell traditional Barbadian products like ceramics, woodcarvings, basketry, and more.

Oistins Fish Market:

The Oistins Fish Market offers an area where you may discover regional artisans selling their original artwork and mementoes, even though it is mostly known for its fresh seafood. Particularly on Friday nights when the Oistins Fish Fry is held, the market is lively and busy.

Earthworks Pottery:

Visit Earthworks Pottery in St. Thomas if you have any interest in pottery or ceramics. They provide exquisitely handcrafted pottery, such as mugs, plates, vases, and more, that makes wonderful gifts.

Local galleries for art:

Barbados has a booming art culture, and the island is home to many galleries where you may find one-of-a-kind creations by regional artists. The works of talented Barbadian artists are on display in venues like the Barbados Gallery of Art and the Zemicon Gallery in Bridgetown.

Rum:

Consider purchasing a bottle or two of rum from Barbados as a memento. There are several rum distilleries on the island, including Mount Gay Rum, Foursquare Rum Distillery, and St. Nicholas Abbey, where you can find out how rum is made and buy several kinds to take home.

Local Food and Spices:

Don't forget to browse the neighbourhood markets to find a variety of fresh foods, spices, and locally produced foods. One such market is Cheapside Market in Bridgetown. These make wonderfully scrumptious and genuine gifts to send home.

Additional alternatives for shopping and purchasing mementoes in Barbados include:

Barbadian Rum Cakes:

These mouthwatering cakes, a Barbados speciality, are a lovely gift or keepsake. They have a variety of flavours, including chocolate, coconut, and classic fruitcake, and are produced using local rum. On the entire island, you can find them at a lot of grocery stores and gift shops.

Local Art and Crafts Markets:

There are numerous art and craft markets in Barbados where regional artisans sell their handmade goods. The Brighton Farmers Market, Holders Farmers Market, and Hastings Farmers Market are a few examples. A large variety of handcrafted jewellery, apparel, original artwork, and other rare products are available at these markets.

Fashion and Swimwear:
In several boutiques and shopping centres in Barbados, you may buy fashionable swimwear, resort wear, and designer clothing. Popular high-end shopping location Limegrove Lifestyle Centre in Holetown is well-known for its trendy retailers.

Local Spices and Condiments:
By purchasing regional spices, hot sauces, and condiments, you may bring a taste of Barbados' delectable food back home. Look for ingredients that will give your meal a delectable Caribbean flair, such as Bajan seasoning, pepper sauce, and hot pepper jelly.

Local Art and Photography:
Barbados boasts a thriving art scene if you're seeking original artwork or photographs to decorate your walls. Discover a broad variety of artwork, including paintings, sculptures, and photographs that capture the allure of the island, by visiting nearby art studios and galleries.

Barbadian Fashion Designers:
By purchasing local designers' goods, you help support Barbados' expanding fashion community. Look for boutiques and shops that sell items such as jewellery, accessories, and apparel that are designed by Barbadian fashion houses.

Duty-Free Shopping:
Duty-free shopping is very popular in Barbados, especially for high-end goods like jewellery, watches, gadgets, and

designer labels. Duty-free stores are available at the island's international airport, Bridgetown, and a few chosen retail malls.

Before buying anything, always remember to evaluate pricing and quality, especially for pricey things. Additionally, keep a look out for regional celebrations and events where you can discover pop-up markets or artist exhibits with interesting shopping options. Enjoy discovering Barbados' shopping scene!

Here is guidance on how to travel by car or foot to the indicated Barbados shopping and souvenir locations:

Bridgetown:

You can either drive or utilise public transport to arrive to Bridgetown, the capital of Barbados. You can use major thoroughfares like the ABC Highway (Highway 7) or the Spring Garden Highway (Highway 1) if you're driving. In Bridgetown, there are parking lots, but pay attention to the parking regulations.

Chattel Village:

On Barbados' west coast, in the hamlet of Holetown, is where you can find Chattel Village. Drive towards Holetown on the Spring Garden Highway (Highway 1). Once you get to Holetown, Chattel Village is simple to locate and close to the main road. Alternatively, you can travel to Holetown via bus or cab.

Pelican Craft Centre:

Bridgetown's Pelican Craft Centre is located close to the harbour. If you're driving, you can use the earlier-mentioned routes to get to Bridgetown. When you arrive at Bridgetown, use the harbour area's navigation to find the Pelican Craft Centre. Nearby parking choices are available.

Oistins Fish Market:

On Barbados' southern coast, in the community of Oistins, is the Oistins Fish Market. If you're travelling by car, you can merge onto the Christ Church Bypass Road (Highway 5) in the direction of Oistins from the ABC Highway (Highway 7). Although there is parking close to the fish market, it may get busy, particularly on Friday nights.

Earthworks Pottery:
The location of Earthworks Pottery is at St. Thomas, which is inland from Barbados' west coast. If you're driving, you can leave Bridgetown on Highway 2A and keep going until you come to the St. Thomas region. The Earthworks Pottery has its parking area and is situated along the main road.

Local Art Galleries:
Barbados has many art galleries in or near Bridgetown, however, they are dispersed all over the island. The most practical way to get to these galleries is by car or cab. To find certain galleries, it is best to utilise GPS or navigational aids as they may have different addresses and locations.

Rum Distilleries:
There are several rum distilleries on the island of Barbados, including Mount Gay Rum, Foursquare Rum Distillery, and St. Nicholas Abbey. For a convenient visit, it is advised to rent a car or call a cab. The addresses and detailed directions for each distillery are listed on their separate websites.

Barbadian Rum Cakes:
Visit several supermarkets, gift shops and speciality shops across the island to find Barbadian rum cakes. These are usually simple to get to by automobile. A variety of rum cakes are available at supermarkets such as Massy Stores, Super Centre, and Emerald City. Additionally, you might

inquire about nearby rum cake-specific bakeries and confectioneries.

Local Art and Crafts Markets:
Popular marketplaces in Barbados where regional craftsmen sell their wares include Brighton Farmers Market, Holders Farmers Market, and Hastings Farmers Market. Holders Farmers Market is at St. James, Hastings Farmers Market is in Christ Church, and Brighton Farmers Market is in St. George. These markets are typically accessible by automobile, and there are parking opportunities close by.

Fashion and Swimwear:
You can drive to Limegrove Lifestyle Centre in Holetown, which has a variety of stylish retailers. You may get to Holetown on Barbados' west coast by using the Spring Garden Highway (Highway 1) and following the directions. Parking spaces are available at Limegrove Lifestyle Centre.

Local condiments and spices:
Supermarkets, specialist food shops and neighbourhood markets can all be found in the island's native spices, hot sauces and condiments. Popular supermarkets that sell a range of regional goods include Massy Stores, Super Centre, and Emerald City. In Bridgetown, Cheapside Market is a fantastic spot to look around for fresh food and spices.

Local photography and art:
All around the island, but especially in and around Bridgetown, are local art galleries and studios. To go to these venues, which may be dispersed over several areas, it is advised to drive or use a taxi. You can use GPS or navigation tools to find particular galleries using their addresses.

Barbadian fashion designers:
The greatest places to look for boutiques and shops selling items manufactured by Barbadian fashion designers are Holetown, Bridgetown, and other well-known tourist destinations. These places are easily reachable by automobile, and you can use navigational tools to identify particular stores or ask locals for advice.

Duty-Free shopping:
Duty-free shops can be located around the island, including at the Grantley Adams International Airport and in malls and retail centres. The airport is conveniently reachable by vehicle, and malls and retail centres are frequently found in well-known cities and popular tourist destinations. These locations have parking facilities.

Zemicon Gallery and the Barbados Gallery of Art:
The Barbados Gallery of Art may be found in Bridgetown, the island nation's capital. It is located close to the Garrison Historic Area on the outskirts of the city. If you're travelling by car, take the route to Bridgetown and then follow the signs for the Garrison neighbourhood. Parking facilities may be close by and the gallery is easily reachable by vehicle.

Additionally in Bridgetown, more specifically in the Pelican Village complex, is the Zemicon Gallery. Follow the directions to Bridgetown if you're driving, then turn towards the harbour area. The gallery is located inside the complex of Pelican Village, which is close to the harbour. There might be parking opportunities.

Public transport is also available to get to both galleries. In Bridgetown, buses and taxis are widely available, and you can ask residents or the driver for advice or directions to ensure you get to the galleries.

Remember to consider traffic conditions, parking availability, and local driving regulations when travelling by car. It's always a good idea to have a map or use navigation tools to ensure a smooth journey. Enjoy exploring the shopping and souvenir options in Barbados!

Please note that when trekking or walking to these locations, it's essential to consider the distance, road safety, and weather conditions. Barbados is a relatively small island, but walking long distances may not be practical for all locations, especially if they are spread out. Using transportation options like taxis, buses, or renting a car is generally more efficient for exploring the island and reaching these destinations

Barbados Nightlife and Entertainment

For both travellers and visitors, Barbados has a thriving and dynamic nightlife and entertainment scene.
Here are some well-liked choices to consider:
St. Lawrence Gap:
St. Lawrence Gap, which is on Barbados' south coast, is well-known for its vibrant nightlife. Numerous bars, clubs, and eateries that provide live music, DJs, and dancing line the area. From reggae and soca to jazz and world music, everything is available.
Bridgetown:
Bridgetown, the capital of Barbados, is home to a vibrant nightlife. You can go to the vibrant Careenage waterfront

district, which has bars, restaurants, and nightclubs. The 2nd Street neighbourhood is well known for its nightlife, featuring a variety of bars and clubs that cater to all preferences.

Oistins Fish Fry:
The renowned Oistins Fish Fry brings the fishing community of Oistins to life every Friday night. Both locals and visitors go to this event to take in the delectable seafood, lively ambience, music, and dancing. It's a fantastic location for interacting with locals and learning about Bajan culture.

Rum shops:
Rum is famous in Barbados, and going to a rum shop is a must-do Bajan experience. These neighbourhood bars provide a relaxed setting where you may partake in a range of rum-based beverages, listen to music, and strike up conversations with locals. On some nights, live music performances are also held in some rum stores.

Beach Bars:
Many beach bars in Barbados provide a special fusion of breathtaking ocean views, delectable cocktails, and exciting entertainment. You may unwind, take in the sunset, and dance to the sounds of local and foreign musicians at places like Mullins Beach Bar, The Cliff Beach Club, and Nikki Beach Barbados.

Crop Over Festival:
You must not miss the Crop Over Festival if you happen to be in Barbados from June to August. This annual event showcases the island's diverse cultural heritage with colourful parades, calypso music, steel bands, costume contests, and parties.

Harbour Lights:

Harbour Lights is a well-liked beachfront nightclub and entertainment location on Barbados' west coast. Themed party nights, live music, DJs, and exhibits by regional artists are all available. You may enjoy a magnificent beach backdrop while dancing the night away.

Mount Gay Rum Distillery:

A trip to the Mount Gay Rum Distillery is essential for anybody interested in the creation and history of rum. Learn about the rum-making process on a tour of the distillery, sample various rums and unwind with a drink at the on-site bar.

Dinner Shows:

Several locations in Barbados provide supper performances that pair delicious food with live entertainment. While being delighted by skilled performers displaying Bajan music, dance, and cultural performances, you may savour a delectable dinner. The supper shows at The Plantation Theatre and Pirate's Cove is well-known.

Casinos:

Try your luck at one of the Barbados casinos if you're feeling lucky. The Barbados Casino in Christ Church is the most well-known casino. It offers a variety of gambling alternatives, including roulette, blackjack, and slot machines.

Live Music Events:

Live music performances are happening all across the island of Barbados, where the music culture is growing. Watch for live performances by regional and worldwide performers at concerts, jazz nights, and other events. Each year, the Holetown Festival and the Barbados Jazz Festival both feature top musicians.

Sports bars:

You may watch your favourite sporting events in one of the sports bars in Barbados if you're a sports fan. These places provide large displays, energetic settings, and the option to support your team while sipping a cold beverage.

Here's a brief guide on how to get to each of the mentioned places, either by car or on foot:

St. Lawrence Gap: St. Lawrence Gap is located on the south coast of Barbados, and it stretches along Highway 7. If you have a car, you can drive along the highway and easily access the area. It's about a 15-20 minute drive from Bridgetown, depending on traffic. If you prefer to walk, it's possible to reach St. Lawrence Gap from nearby accommodations or the surrounding areas but be prepared for a longer walk.

Bridgetown: Bridgetown is the capital city of Barbados and is located on the southwestern coast of the island. It is easily accessible by car and has parking facilities available in various areas. If you prefer to explore on foot, you can stroll through the city centre and visit the Careenage waterfront area, which is within walking distance from the main shopping districts.

Oistins Fish Fry: Oistins is situated on the south coast of Barbados. If you have a car, you can take the ABC Highway (Highway 6) and then head south on Highway 7 to reach Oistins. It's approximately a 20-25 minute drive from Bridgetown. If you're in the nearby area of Worthing or St. Lawrence Gap, you can also reach Oistins by foot along the coast, which would take about 30-40 minutes.

Rum Shops: Rum shops can be found throughout Barbados, including in various towns and villages. It's best to ask locals for recommendations on nearby rum shops based on your location. If you have a car, you can easily drive to the nearest rum shop. Alternatively, some rum shops are within walking distance from popular tourist areas.

Beach Bars: The beach bars mentioned, such as Mullins Beach Bar, The Cliff Beach Club, and Nikki Beach Barbados, are located on the west coast of Barbados. If you have a car, you can drive along coastal Highway 1 and find parking near the respective beach bars. If you're staying in a nearby hotel or resort, it may be possible to walk to some of these beach bars.

Crop Over Festival: The Crop Over Festival takes place at various locations across the island of Barbados. Major events are held in Bridgetown, including the Grand Kadooment parade. You can reach Bridgetown by car or public transportation, and from there, follow the directions provided for Bridgetown.

Harbour Lights: Harbour Lights is located on the outskirts of Bridgetown, specifically in the Bay Street area. It's easily accessible by car, and there are parking options nearby. If you're staying in the city centre, you can also walk to Harbour Lights, as it's within walking distance from downtown Bridgetown.

Mount Gay Rum Distillery: The Mount Gay Rum Distillery is located in St. Lucy, in the northern part of the island. It's about a 30-40 minute drive from Bridgetown. If you have a car, you can take Highway 1B and then head north on Highway 2 to reach the distillery. There's a parking lot available on-site.

Dinner Shows: The Plantation Theatre and Pirate's Cove are located on the west coast of Barbados. If you have a car, you can drive along coastal Highway 1 and find parking near the respective venues. Alternatively, some accommodations may offer transportation services to these dinner show locations.

Casinos: The Barbados Casino is located in Christ Church, specifically in the St. Lawrence Gap area. It's easily accessible by car, and there are parking options available nearby. If you prefer to walk, and you're staying in the St. Lawrence Gap area, you can easily reach the casino on foot.

Live Music Events: Live music events take place at various venues across the island, so the directions will depend on the specific location of the event. It's best to check event listings or ask locals for directions to the venue you're interested in attending. If you have a car, you can use GPS or navigation apps to find your way. If you're in the Bridgetown area, many live music events take place in the city centre, making them easily accessible on foot.

Sports Bars: Sports bars are scattered across Barbados, including in Bridgetown and other towns. To find a sports bar near your location, you can ask locals or check online directories. If you have a car, you can drive to the sports bar of your choice. Alternatively, if you're staying in the area, you can walk to sports bars located within your vicinity.

Remember to consider traffic conditions, parking availability, and local regulations while driving in Barbados. If you choose to walk, make sure to stay on well-lit and safe routes, especially at night. It's always a good idea to plan your route, use navigation tools, or ask for directions to ensure a smooth and enjoyable experience getting to each destination.

Best place to eat, drink and chop in Barbados

Barbados is known for its vibrant culinary scene, offering a variety of delicious food and drink options for travellers and tourists.

Here are some of the best places to eat, drink, and shop in Barbados, along with directions for locating each either by car or on foot:

Oistins Fish Fry (Oistins, Christ Church)

Oistins Fish Fry

Oistins Fish Fry is a must-visit spot for seafood lovers. It's a lively open-air market where you can sample freshly caught fish, grilled or fried, along with local side dishes.

You can get there by car from Bridgetown by taking Highway 7 towards Oistins or by foot if you're staying nearby.

The Cliff (Derricks, St. James)

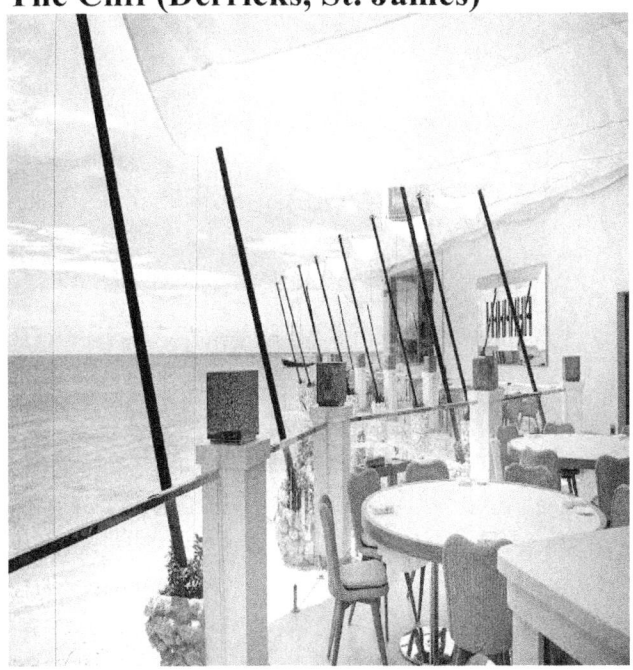

The Cliff (Derricks, St. James)

The Cliff is an upscale oceanfront restaurant known for its stunning views and gourmet cuisine. It offers a fine dining experience with a fusion of Caribbean and international flavours. To reach The Cliff, you can drive north from Bridgetown along Highway 1, and it's located in Derricks, St. James.

Mount Gay Visitor Centre (Bridgetown, St. Michael)

Mount Gay Visitor Centre (Bridgetown, St. Michael)
If you're a rum enthusiast, a visit to the Mount Gay Visitor Centre is a must. It's the oldest rum distillery in the world, offering tours and tastings that delve into the history and production of Barbados' famous Mount Gay Rum. The visitor centre is located in Bridgetown, St. Michael, and you can reach it by car or foot, depending on your location.
Cuz's Fish Shack (Pebbles Beach, Bridgetown)

Cuz's Fish Shack (Pebbles Beach, Bridgetown)
Cuz's Fish Shack is a popular local eatery situated right on Pebbles Beach. They serve mouthwatering fish sandwiches, wraps, and other seafood dishes at affordable prices. It's a great spot to enjoy tasty food with a view of the Caribbean Sea. You can reach Cuz's Fish Shack by car or foot, as it's located in Bridgetown.
St. Lawrence Gap (Christ Church)

St. Lawrence Gap (Christ Church)
St. Lawrence Gap is a lively area in Christ Church filled with numerous restaurants, bars, and nightclubs. It's a hub for nightlife in Barbados, offering a wide range of dining options, from casual to fine dining. To get there by car, take Highway 7 and head south from Bridgetown. Alternatively, you can reach St. Lawrence Gap on foot if you're staying nearby.
Cheapside Market (Bridgetown, St. Michael)

Cheapside Market (Bridgetown, St. Michael)
If you're looking to experience the local flavours and fresh produce, Cheapside Market is the place to go. It's a bustling market in Bridgetown where you can find a variety of fruits, vegetables, spices, and local delicacies. It's situated in Bridgetown, St. Michael, and you can easily access it by car or foot.
Cuz's Fish Shack (Carlisle Bay, Bridgetown)

Cuz's Fish Shack (Carlisle Bay, Bridgetown)
Another branch of Cuz's Fish Shack is located on Carlisle Bay, near Bridgetown. This beachfront spot offers delicious fish dishes, including their famous fish cutter sandwiches. It's a great place to relax, enjoy the beach, and savour some tasty seafood. You can reach Cuz's Fish Shack at Carlisle Bay by car or foot.
Brown Sugar Restaurant (Aquatic Gap, St. Michael)

Brown Sugar Restaurant (Aquatic Gap, St. Michael)
Brown Sugar Restaurant is known for its delectable Bajan buffet-style meals. It offers an array of local dishes like flying fish, macaroni pie, and plantains. The restaurant has a cosy ama Cosy located in Aquatic Gap, St. Michael. You can easily reach it by car or foot from Bridgetown.
Shakers Bar & Grill (Hastings, Christ Church)

Shakers Bar & Grill (Hastings, Christ Church)
Shakers Bar & Grill is a popular sports bar located in Hastings, Christ Church. It's a great place to enjoy a casual meal, watch sports events, and socialize with locals and fellow travellers. They serve a variety of dishes, including burgers, wings, and seafood. Shakers Bar & Grill is easily accessible by car or foot.
Limegrove Lifestyle Centre (Holetown, St. James)

Limegrove Lifestyle Centre (Holetown, St. James)
For those looking for a shopping experience, Limegrove Lifestyle Centre is a premier shopping destination in Barbados. It features a mix of international luxury brands, boutique shops, and restaurants. Limegrove is located in Holetown, St. James, and you can easily reach it by car from Bridgetown or by foot if you're staying nearby.
Just Grillin' (Rockley, Christ Church)

Just Grillin' (Rockley, Christ Church)
Just Grillin' is a popular restaurant that offers a variety of grilled dishes, including fish, chicken, and burgers. They focus on using fresh, locally sourced ingredients. Just Grillin' has multiple locations in Barbados, including Rockley, and Christ Church, which you can reach by car or foot.
The Tides Restaurant (Holetown, St. James)

The Tides Restaurant (Holetown, St. James)
The Tides Restaurant is an elegant beachfront restaurant known for its exquisite cuisine and picturesque setting. They offer a blend of Caribbean and international flavours, and their menu features a selection of seafood, meats, and vegetarian dishes. The Tides Restaurant is located in Holetown, St. James, and can be reached by car or foot.

These recommendations will give you a diverse taste of the culinary offerings in Barbados and provide opportunities to explore different parts of the island. Enjoy your dining, drinking, and shopping experiences in Barbados!

Here is some general information about the opening hours of the mentioned establishments:

Oistins Fish Fry: The Oistins Fish Fry is typically open on Friday and Saturday evenings, starting around 7:00 PM and continuing late into the night.

The Cliff: The Cliff is a fine dining restaurant that usually opens for dinner service from around 6:30 PM. It is recommended to make reservations in advance.

Mount Gay Visitor Centre: The Mount Gay Visitor Centre usually operates from Monday to Saturday, with tours and tastings available throughout the day. It's best to check their website or contact them for specific opening hours.

Cuz's Fish Shack (Pebbles Beach): Cuz's Fish Shack is generally open for lunch and dinner service. They usually operate from mid-morning until late evening, but it's advisable to confirm their exact hours of operation.

St. Lawrence Gap: The restaurants, bars, and nightclubs in St. Lawrence Gap have varying opening hours. Generally, restaurants are open for dinner service, and bars and nightclubs tend to open later in the evening, with some staying open until the early hours of the morning.

Cheapside Market: Cheapside Market is typically open from Monday to Saturday, starting early in the morning and closing in the early afternoon. It's best to visit in the morning for the widest variety of fresh produce.

Cuz's Fish Shack (Carlisle Bay): Cuz's Fish Shack location on Carlisle Bay usually operates during the day, serving lunch and early dinner. Opening hours may vary, so it's recommended to check with them directly.

Brown Sugar Restaurant: Brown Sugar Restaurant typically opens for lunch and dinner service. They may have specific hours for each mealtime, so it's advisable to confirm their opening hours in advance.

Shakers Bar & Grill: Shakers Bar & Grill is primarily open in the evenings, with hours extending into the night. It's a popular spot for watching sports events and socializing.

Limegrove Lifestyle Centre: Limegrove Lifestyle Centre usually opens around 10:00 AM and closes in the evening. The shopping centre's hours may vary slightly for different stores and restaurants within the complex.

Just Grillin': Just Grillin' locations are generally open for lunch and dinner service. They typically open around mid-morning and close in the late evening.

The Tides Restaurant: The Tides Restaurant is typically open for dinner service, starting around 6:00 PM. Reservations are recommended, especially during peak tourist seasons.

Please remember that these are general guidelines, and it's essential to confirm the specific opening hours and availability of each place before visiting, as they may be subject to change or have different operating schedules depending on the season or specific circumstances.

Water sports and Activities in Barbados

Barbados, known for its stunning beaches and crystal-clear waters, offers a wide range of water sports and activities for travellers and tourists.

Here are some popular options:

Snorkelling and Scuba Diving: Explore the vibrant coral reefs and underwater life in Barbados. There are numerous diving and snorkelling spots, such as Carlisle Bay Marine Park, Folkestone Marine Park, and the SS Stavronikita shipwreck.

Jet Skiing: Rent a jet ski and enjoy the thrill of speeding across the waves along the coast of Barbados. Jet ski rentals are available at various beaches and water sports centres.

Surfing: Barbados is a surfer's paradise, attracting wave enthusiasts from around the world. Popular surf spots include Soup Bowl in Bathsheba, Freights Bay, and Brandon's Beach. Surf schools and rentals are available for beginners and experienced surfers alike.

Stand-Up Paddleboarding (SUP): Glide along the calm waters of Barbados on a paddleboard. SUP is a great way to explore the coastline, enjoy the scenery, and even try some yoga or fitness routines on the water.

Catamaran Cruises: Embark on a catamaran cruise and sail along the picturesque coastline of Barbados. These cruises often include snorkelling, swimming with sea turtles, and stopping at beautiful beaches. Some catamaran tours also offer delicious food and drinks on board.

Kayaking: Paddle your way through the calm bays, mangroves, and scenic coastlines of Barbados. Kayaking tours are available, allowing you to explore the island's natural beauty and observe marine life up close.

Fishing: Barbados is renowned for its fishing opportunities. Join a deep-sea fishing charter and try your hand at catching marlin, tuna, wahoo, or mahi-mahi. Fishing trips can be arranged for both experienced anglers and beginners.

Sailing: Experience the joy of sailing in Barbados. You can rent a small sailboat or join a sailing excursion to enjoy the Caribbean waters, gentle breezes, and stunning views of the coastline.

Kitesurfing and Windsurfing: Barbados' consistent trade winds make it an ideal destination for kitesurfing and windsurfing. Silver Sands and Long Beach are popular spots for these thrilling water sports.

Water Skiing and Wakeboarding: If you're looking for some adrenaline-pumping action, try water skiing or wakeboarding. Various water sports centres offer rentals and lessons for beginners and experienced riders.

Remember to prioritize your safety while participating in water sports and activities. It's advisable to follow any guidelines provided by the operators and be aware of the local weather conditions and regulations.

Here are directions on how to locate each water sport and activity mentioned in Barbados, either by car or foot:

Snorkelling and Scuba Diving:

Carlisle Bay Marine Park: Located on the southwest coast of Barbados, near Bridgetown. You can drive there by taking Highway 7 (Bridgetown to St. Lawrence Gap) and following signs to Carlisle Bay.

Folkestone Marine Park: Situated in Holetown on the west coast. You can reach it by driving along Highway 1 (West Coast Road) and following signs to Holetown.

Jet Skiing:

Jet ski rentals are available at various beaches, including popular spots like Dover Beach in St. Lawrence Gap, Mullins Beach in Mullins, and Accra Beach in Rockley.

Surfing:

Soup Bowl (Bathsheba): Located on the east coast. You can drive there by taking Highway 5 (ABC Highway) and then following signs to Bathsheba.

Freights Bay: Situated in Christ Church, near Oistins. You can reach it by driving along Highway 7 (Bridgetown to St. Lawrence Gap) and following signs to Oistins.

Brandon's Beach: Found in Bridgetown on the southwest coast. It's within walking distance from the city centre.

Stand-Up Paddleboarding (SUP):

Rentals and tours for SUP are available at various beaches, including Dover Beach, Carlisle Bay, and Pebbles Beach.

Catamaran Cruises:

Catamaran cruises typically depart from the marinas in Bridgetown or Holetown. The exact departure points may vary depending on the tour operator. It's recommended to book a cruise in advance and check the departure location with the operator.

Kayaking:

Kayaking tours are offered at various locations, such as Carlisle Bay, Folkestone Marine Park, and the waters around Bridgetown. It's best to book a tour in advance and confirm the meeting point with the operator.

Fishing:

Deep-sea fishing charters can be arranged from the marinas in Bridgetown or Holetown. Contact fishing charter companies in advance to book your trip and confirm the departure location.

Sailing:

Small sailboat rentals and sailing excursions are available at marinas in Bridgetown or Holetown. Contact sailing operators in advance to arrange your sailing experience and confirm the departure location.

Kitesurfing and Windsurfing:

Silver Sands: Located on the south coast, near Oistins. You can drive there by taking Highway 7 (Bridgetown to St. Lawrence Gap) and following signs to Oistins.

Long Beach: Situated on the southeast coast. You can drive there by taking Highway 5 (ABC Highway) and then following signs to Long Beach.

Water Skiing and Wakeboarding:
Water sports centres offering water skiing and wakeboarding rentals are often found at popular beaches like Dover Beach, Accra Beach, and Mullins Beach. Contact the water sports centres in advance to confirm the availability and location.

Please note that it's always recommended to use GPS navigation or local maps for precise directions and to check with local authorities or tourism offices for any updates or specific instructions related to the locations and activities.

How to live on a budget in Barbados

With some thoughtful planning and wise decisions, travelling on a budget in Barbados is doable. Here are some suggestions to help you maximise your funds while having fun in Barbados:

Accommodation:
Instead of lavish resorts, think about staying in more affordable lodging options like guesthouses, hostels, or self-catering apartments. Affordably priced solutions can

be found in places like Christ Church or St. James. Look online for offers and discounts, or think about making a reservation through a local vacation rental company.

Transportation:

Avoid costly private taxis by using shared taxis (sometimes referred to as "ZR vans") and other forms of public transit. The cheapest alternative is by bus, which has lines that circle the entire island. ZR vans cost a little more, but they have a more flexible schedule.

Eating and Dining:

For more affordable real Bajan food, seek out neighbourhood restaurants and street food vendors. These restaurants frequently serve mouthwatering regional cuisine like flying fish, cou-cou, or fish cakes. You may buy snacks, fresh fruits, and other products at supermarkets and grocery stores, enabling you to prepare your meals at home and save money on eating out.

Free Activities and Beaches:

Beautiful beaches may be found in Barbados, and fortunately, using them is free. Spend your days swimming, tanning, and lounging on the stunning beaches. Explore the island's natural attractions as well, such as the Animal Flower Cave and Hunte's Gardens, which occasionally charge no admission at all.

Activities and Water Sports:

There are inexpensive alternatives to several of the more expensive water activities. Find local businesses that charge inexpensive prices for sports like kayaking, paddleboarding, and snorkelling. To get better deals, think about haggling over rates or reserving numerous activities with the same company.

Entertainment at night:

Check out neighbourhood pubs and bars that offer happy hour deals or live music performances to save money on entertainment. Be aware that some businesses may impose a cover fee. Look for local events, such as festivals or cultural celebrations, which frequently offer free or inexpensive admittance.

Shopping:
Avoid tourist locations where prices tend to be higher if you like to shop. Instead, go to local marketplaces like Cheapside Market or Bridgetown Market, where you may buy cheaper fresh food, regional handicrafts, and mementoes. Never forget to bargain for better prices!

island excursion:
Investigate the island on your own rather than paying for pricey guided tours. Rent a car or take the bus to independently explore well-known sites like Bathsheba, Harrison's Cave, or the Barbados Wildlife Reserve.

Change of Currencies:
Be aware of currency conversion costs. To achieve the best exchange rates, it is frequently preferable to exchange your money in advance or to withdraw cash from an ATM. Avoid changing money at airports or hotels because the exchange rates there are typically not as good.

Study and Prepare in Advance:
Do some research on the local restaurants, activities, and events that will be taking place while you are there before you go. This will enable you to make the most of your time in Barbados without going overboard with your spending.

Keep in mind that enjoying Barbados' natural beauty and rich culture doesn't have to come at the expense of your financial situation. You may have a fun and economical trip by making wise decisions and looking for low-cost options.

et Travel Barbados

User

Travellers and tourists How to live on a budget in Barbados

ChatGPT

Living on a budget while travelling in Barbados is possible with careful planning and smart choices. Here are some tips to help you make the most of your money while enjoying your time in Barbados:

Accommodation: Consider staying in budget-friendly accommodations such as guesthouses, hostels, or self-catering apartments instead of high-end resorts. You can find affordable options in areas like Christ Church or St. James. Look for deals and discounts online or consider booking through local vacation rental websites.

Transportation: Opt for public transportation like buses and shared taxis (known as "ZR vans") instead of expensive private taxis. Buses are the most cost-effective option, with routes covering the entire island. ZR vans are a bit more expensive but offer a more flexible schedule.

Food and Dining: Look for local eateries and street food vendors to experience authentic Bajan cuisine at lower prices. These places often offer delicious local dishes like flying fish, cou-cou, or fish cakes. Supermarkets and grocery stores are great for buying snacks, fresh fruits, and other groceries, allowing you to prepare your meals and save money on dining out.

Beaches and Free Activities: Barbados is known for its stunning beaches, and fortunately, enjoying them is free! Spend your days soaking up the sun, swimming, and relaxing on the beautiful shores. Additionally, explore the island's natural attractions like the Animal Flower Cave or

Hunte's Gardens, which have minimal entry fees or sometimes even free.

Water Sports and Activities: While some water sports can be quite expensive, there are affordable options available. Look for local vendors who offer activities like snorkelling, paddleboarding, or kayaking at reasonable rates. Consider negotiating prices or booking multiple activities with the same provider to get better deals.

Nightlife and Entertainment: To save money on entertainment, check out local bars and pubs that offer happy hour specials or live music performances. Some establishments may have cover charges, so be mindful of that. Look for events happening in the area, such as festivals or cultural celebrations, which often have free or low-cost entry.

Shopping: If you're interested in shopping, avoid touristy areas where prices tend to be higher. Instead, visit local markets like Cheapside Market or Bridgetown Market, where you can find fresh produce, local crafts, and souvenirs at more affordable prices. Don't forget to haggle for better deals!

Island Tours: Instead of expensive guided tours, explore the island independently. Rent a car or use public transportation to visit popular attractions like Harrison's Cave, Bathsheba, or the Barbados Wildlife Reserve at your own pace.

Currency Exchange: Be mindful of currency exchange rates and fees. It's often better to exchange your money in advance or withdraw cash from ATMs to get the best rates. Avoid exchanging currency at airports or hotels, as they usually offer less favourable rates.

Research and Plan Ahead: Before your trip, research free or low-cost attractions, dining options, and local events taking place during your visit. This will help you plan your budget accordingly and make the most of your time in Barbados without overspending.

Remember, living on a budget in Barbados doesn't mean you have to compromise on experiencing the island's beauty and culture. By making smart choices and seeking out affordable options, you can have an enjoyable and cost-effective trip.

User

List out the budget-friendly accommodation and how to locate each either by car or foot

List out where they can get cheap food at lower prices and directions to reach each one either by car or

For the nightlife and activities list local bars and pubs that offer happy hour specials or live music performances and directions to each one either by car or foot

Here are some budget-friendly accommodations, affordable food options, and local bars/pubs with happy hour specials or live music performances in Barbados:

Budget-Friendly Accommodation:
- Rostrevor Hotel (Location: St. Lawrence Gap, Christ Church) - Accessible by car or foot.

By Car: From Bridgetown, head southeast on Highway 7. Continue on Highway 7 until you reach St. Lawrence Gap. The Rostrevor Hotel will be on your left.

By Foot: St. Lawrence Gap is a pedestrian-friendly area, and the Rostrevor Hotel is easily accessible on foot once you reach St. Lawrence Gap.

Rostrevor Hotel
- Dover Beach Hotel (Location: St. Lawrence Gap, Christ Church) - Accessible by car or foot.

By Car: Follow the same directions as above to St. Lawrence Gap. The Dover Beach Hotel is located along the gap, and you can park in the nearby parking areas.

By Foot: St. Lawrence Gap is a pedestrian-friendly area, and the Dover Beach Hotel is easily accessible on foot once you reach St. Lawrence Gap.

Dover Beach Hotel
- Butterfly Beach Hotel (Location: Maxwell Coast Road, Christ Church) - Accessible by car or foot.

By Car: From Bridgetown, head southeast on Highway 7. Continue on Highway 7 until you reach Maxwell Coast Road. Turn left onto Maxwell Coast Road, and the Butterfly Beach Hotel will be on your right.

By Foot: The Butterfly Beach Hotel is within walking distance from St. Lawrence Gap, but it may be a long walk. It's recommended to use a car or public transportation for easier access.

Butterfly Beach Hotel
- Pirate's Inn (Location: Browne's Gap, Christ Church) - Accessible by car or foot.

By Car: From Bridgetown, head southeast on Highway 7. Continue on Highway 7 until you reach Browne's Gap. Turn left onto Browne's Gap, and the Pirate's Inn will be on your left.

By Foot: Browne's Gap is not a pedestrian-friendly area, and it may not be easily accessible on foot. It's recommended to use a car or public transportation.

Pirate's Inn
- Sea-U Guest House (Location: Tent Bay, Bathsheba, St. Joseph) - Accessible by car.

By Car: From Bridgetown, head east on Highway 1. Continue on Highway 1 until you reach Bathsheba. In Bathsheba, turn right onto Foster Hall Road, which leads to Tent Bay. The Sea-U Guest House will be on your right in Tent Bay.

By Foot: Tent Bay is a small area, and the Sea-U Guest House is easily accessible on foot once you reach Tent Bay.

Sea-U Guest House
Cheap Food Options:
- Oistins Fish Fry (Location: Oistins, Christ Church) - Accessible by car or foot.
- Cuz's Fish Stand (Location: Pebbles Beach, Bridgetown, St. Michael) - Accessible by car or foot.
- Just Grillin' (Location: Various outlets, including Sunset Crest, St. James) - Accessible by car.
- Jenny's Place (Location: Holetown, St. James) - Accessible by car.
- Chefette (Location: Multiple outlets across the island) - Accessible by car.

Local Bars/Pubs with Happy Hour Specials or Live Music:
- Harbour Lights (Location: Highway 7, Bay Street, St. Michael) - Accessible by car or foot.

- The Waterfront Café (Location: Careenage, Bridgetown, St. Michael) - Accessible by car or foot.
- The Gap (St. Lawrence Gap, Christ Church) - Accessible by car or foot.
- Mullins Beach Bar (Location: Mullins Beach, St. Peter) - Accessible by car.
- John Moore Bar (Location: Weston, St. James) - Accessible by car.

Here are the directions to each of the cheap food options mentioned:

Oistins Fish Fry (Oistins, Christ Church):

By Car: From Bridgetown, head southeast on Highway 7. Continue on Highway 7 until you reach Oistins. Oistins Fish Fry is located near the Oistins Bay Gardens, and there are parking areas available nearby.

By Foot: Oistins Fish Fry is within walking distance from the Oistins area, so it's easily accessible on foot once you reach Oistins.

Cuz's Fish Stand (Pebbles Beach, Bridgetown, St. Michael):

By Car: From Bridgetown, head south on Bay Street until you reach Pebbles Beach. Cuz's Fish Stand is located at Pebbles Beach, and there are parking areas available nearby.

By Foot: Pebbles Beach is within walking distance from Bridgetown, and Cuz's Fish Stand is easily accessible on foot once you reach the beach area.

Just Grillin' (Various outlets, including Sunset Crest, St. James):

By Car: Sunset Crest is located in St. James, just north of Holetown. Use Highway 1 (West Coast Road) and look for the signage to Sunset Crest. There are parking areas available in the area.

By Foot: If you're already in the Sunset Crest or Holetown area, Just Grillin' is easily accessible on foot from there.

Jenny's Place (Holetown, St. James):

By Car: Holetown is located in St. James, along the West Coast. Use Highway 1 (West Coast Road) and look for the signage to Holetown. There are parking areas available in the area.

By Foot: Jenny's Place is located in Holetown, and it's easily accessible on foot from the central area of Holetown.

Chefette (Multiple outlets across the island):

By Car: Chefette has multiple outlets across the island, so the directions will depend on the specific outlet you wish to visit. You can use GPS or online maps to find the nearest Chefette location to your current or desired location.

By Foot: The accessibility of Chefette outlets on foot will depend on their specific locations. Some outlets may be more pedestrian-friendly than others, so it's recommended to check the surroundings and plan accordingly.

Please note that road conditions, traffic, and parking availability can vary, so it's always a good idea to check for the most up-to-date directions using a GPS navigation system or online maps before starting your journey.

Here are the directions to each of the local bars/pubs with happy hour specials or live music mentioned:

Harbour Lights (Highway 7, Bay Street, St. Michael):

By Car: From Bridgetown, head south on Bay Street (Highway 7) until you reach Harbour Lights on the left-hand side. There is parking available nearby.

By Foot: If you're in the central area of Bridgetown, you can walk south on Bay Street (Highway 7) until you reach Harbour Lights.

The Waterfront Café (Careenage, Bridgetown, St. Michael):

By Car: From Bridgetown, head towards the Careenage area. The Waterfront Café is located along the waterfront in Bridgetown, and there are parking areas available nearby.

By Foot: If you're in the central area of Bridgetown, you can easily walk to the Careenage area where The Waterfront Café is located.

The Gap (St. Lawrence Gap, Christ Church):

By Car: From Bridgetown, head southeast on Highway 7 until you reach St. Lawrence Gap. The Gap is a street in the St. Lawrence Gap area, and there are parking areas available in the vicinity.

By Foot: St. Lawrence Gap is a pedestrian-friendly area, and The Gap is easily accessible on foot once you reach St. Lawrence Gap.

Mullins Beach Bar (Mullins Beach, St. Peter):

By Car: From Bridgetown, head north on Highway 1 (West Coast Road) until you reach Mullins Beach in St. Peter. Mullins Beach Bar is located on the beach, and there is parking available nearby.

By Foot: If you're already in the Mullins Beach area, Mullins Beach Bar is easily accessible on foot from the beach.

John Moore Bar (Weston, St. James):

By Car: From Bridgetown, head north on Highway 1 (West Coast Road) until you reach Weston in St. James. John Moore Bar is located in the Weston area, and there is parking available nearby.

By Foot: If you're already in the Weston area, John Moore Bar is easily accessible on foot from there.

Safety and health information

COVID-19 Precautions:
- Check the latest travel advisories and entry requirements before your trip, as they may change frequently.
- Follow all health and safety protocols put in place by the Barbadian authorities, including mask-wearing, social distancing, and hand hygiene.
- Be aware of any testing or vaccination requirements for entry into Barbados, and carry the necessary documentation.
- Stay updated on the local COVID-19 situation and adhere to any restrictions or guidelines implemented by the government.

General Safety:
- Barbados is generally considered a safe destination, but it's always wise to take precautions. Keep an eye on your belongings, especially in crowded tourist areas.
- Avoid isolated or poorly lit areas, particularly at night.

- Use reputable transportation options, such as licensed taxis or recognized ride-sharing services.
- Be cautious when swimming or engaging in water sports, and adhere to any posted warnings or instructions from lifeguards.

Medical Facilities:
- Barbados has modern medical facilities and trained medical professionals.
- It's recommended to have travel insurance that covers medical expenses and emergency evacuation.
- Carry any necessary prescription medications in their original containers and bring copies of your prescriptions.

Natural Hazards:
- Barbados is not prone to major natural disasters. However, during the hurricane season (June to November), there is a possibility of tropical storms or hurricanes. Stay informed about weather conditions and follow any instructions or evacuation notices issued by local authorities.

Sun Safety:
- Barbados has a tropical climate, so it's essential to protect yourself from the sun.
- Use sunscreen with a high SPF, wear protective clothing, and stay hydrated to avoid heatstroke or sunburn.

Consider checking the official website of Barbados Tourism Marketing Inc. and the travel advisories issued by your home country for the most recent guidance.

Here are some specific do's and don'ts to help travellers stay safe in Barbados:

Do's:

- Do research and familiarize yourself with the local laws, customs, and culture of Barbados before your trip.
- Do carry a copy of your passport, identification, and emergency contact information with you at all times.
- Do use reliable transportation options, such as licensed taxis or reputable car rental services.
- Do take precautions to protect yourself from the sun, including wearing sunscreen, a hat, and sunglasses, and seeking shade during peak hours.
- Do drink plenty of bottled water to stay hydrated, especially in the warm climate.
- Do exercise caution when engaging in water activities, such as swimming or snorkelling. snorkel instructions from lifeguards and be aware of any warnings or flags indicating unsafe conditions.
- Do keep an eye on your personal belongings and valuables, especially in crowded areas and tourist hotspots.
- Do respect the local culture and customs, including dress codes for religious sites or more conservative areas.
- Do seek medical assistance if you feel unwell or have any health concerns. Barbados has modern medical facilities and trained professionals to provide the necessary care.
- Do follow any health and safety guidelines and regulations related to COVID-19, including wearing masks, practising social distancing, and sanitizing hands regularly.

Don'ts:
- Don't leave your belongings unattended or display signs of wealth, as it may attract unwanted attention.

- Don't use unlicensed or unauthorized tour operators or transportation services.
- Don't swim alone in unfamiliar areas, particularly if there are no lifeguards present.
- Don't engage in illegal activities, including drug use or possession.
- Don't underestimate the power of the sun. Avoid excessive exposure and sunburn by taking necessary precautions.
- Don't drink tap water unless it has been properly filtered or boiled. Stick to bottled water.
- Don't litter. Respect the environment and dispose of waste properly.
- Don't disrespect or offend the local residents or their cultural practices.
- Don't rely solely on online information. Stay updated with official sources and local authorities for the latest safety and health guidelines.
- Don't neglect travel insurance. Ensure you have adequate coverage for medical emergencies, trip cancellations, or any unforeseen circumstances.

Following these do's and don'ts will help you have a safe and enjoyable experience during your visit to Barbados.

Printed in Great Britain
by Amazon